Editor:

Ina Massler Levin, M.A.

Senior Editor:

Sharon Coan, M.S. Ed.

Art Direction:

Elayne Roberts

Product Manager:

Phil Garcia

Imaging:

Alfred Lau

Cover Artist:

Kathy Bruce

Publishers:

Rachelle Cracchiolo, M.S. Ed.

Mary Dupuy Smith, M.S. Ed.

Learning Through Literature
U.S. HIS

INTERMEDIATE

Author:
Concetta Doti Ryan, M.A.

Illustrator:
Agi S. Palinay

Teacher Created Materials, Inc.

P.O. Box 1040

Huntington Beach, CA   92647

©*1994 Teacher Created Materials, Inc.*

Made in U.S.A.

ISBN-1-55734-472-8

Table of Contents

Table of Contents *(cont.)*

Introduction

Learning Through Literature—U.S. History is a 144-page resource book which provides specific strategies and activities for integrating middle grade elementary history curriculum with 35 related children's literature selections. It addresses two current trends in education: the whole language movement and emphasis on integrating curriculum areas. Whole language philosophy stresses the use of literature to build literacy by connecting content areas. Basic knowledge of history is an essential ingredient in creating world citizens for the future. By using quality children's literature with follow-up activities, students' interest in history can be enhanced effectively.

Learning Through Literature—U.S. History includes the following sections:

Personal History

Discovery of the Americas

Colonization

Westward Expansion

American Revolution

Civil War

World Wars

Vietnam War

Each section contains descriptions of picture books and novels along with a variety of follow-up activities with supporting project and pattern pages. An extensive bibliography for each section lists additional titles appropriate for that area of history study.

Follow-up activities extend and reinforce both the literary and the historic concepts by using various forms of expression including:

Poetry	**Writing**
Art	**Brainstorming**
Cooking	**Critical Thinking**
Dramatics	**Science**
Games	**Math**

The goal of *Learning Through Literature—U.S. History* is to improve instruction in the middle grade elementary classroom by blending history and literature, providing hands-on activities that can easily be implemented, and sparking children's interest in history.

Do People Grow on Family Trees?

Author: Ira Wolfman

Illustrator: Michael Klein

Publisher: Workman Publishing, New York, 1991. 153 pages

Summary: Studying your family's genealogy can be fun with the help of this wonderful resource book. Ira Wolfman's own personal story of becoming an "ancestor detector" is told in this book along with basic training for kids to begin a study of their family history.

Teacher's Note: Please use your own discretion in selecting activities appropriate for the students in your class. This is a personal family history unit which requires students to uncover detailed information about their family.

Learning Activities:

(Introduction)

- Have students use a cluster to brainstorm the reasons why they might want to become "ancestor detectors."

(Chapter 1)

- You may wish to put the three basic genealogical rules on chart paper in your classroom. These rules can be found on page 6 of *Do People Grow on Family Trees?*.
- Read several of the personal stories of people finding out about their family history located in chapter one of *Do People Grow on Family Trees?*.

(Chapter 2)

- On page 21 of *Do People Grow on Family Trees?* a sidebox provides a discussion of immigrants remembering the "old country." Have students write letters to pretend family members in the "old country" describing what it is like to be a recent immigrant in the United States.

Do People Grow on Family Trees? *(cont.)*

- Have students debate whether or not the "doors to America should be closed." Pages 28-29 of *Do People Grow on Family Trees?* provides basic information regarding the controversy. You may wish to make this a current event project because newspapers often print stories about immigrants.

- Depending on the background of your group, have students try to find out who was their first relative to immigrate to the United States. Then have them fill out the melting pot pattern on page 9 indicating the first family member to reach America, the date, and where that family member came from. These "pots" can be used to make a classroom bulletin board. If students cannot find this information let them choose any relative who immigrated.

(Chapter 3)

- As students begin their study of the past, have them interview their closest relatives, (i.e. parents and grandparents), using the interview sheet located on pages 10-11. Encourage students to purchase a binder or notebook in which to keep all their research throughout this family history project.

- Students should become well acquainted with their own personal history. They may begin by answering the questions on pages 11-12. Again, they should keep these notes in their notebook or binder.

- If students have gathered enough information in their interviews, they may want to begin filling out the pedigree chart. A sample pedigree chart can be found on page 36 of *Do People Grow on Family Trees?*. Blanks are available on page 162 of the book.

- If students are interested in making a family tree they may wish to write for this special publication: "The Living Family Tree." This publication offers suggestions for making unusual family trees. For a copy of the booklet, students may write to Marie Schreiner, 2709 Lamplighter Lane, Minneapolis, MN 55422. The family tree makes a nice gift for someone special.

- If the pedigree chart is too complicated for students, you may wish to have them use the family group sheet to record information. A sample is located on page 38 of *Do People Grow on Family Trees?*. A blank is located on page 163 of the book.

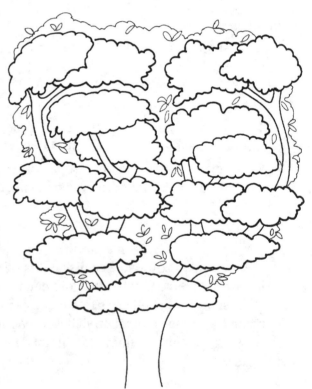

(Chapter 4)

- Have students write a sensory descriptive piece of what it may have been like for immigrants to see the Statue of Liberty for the first time.

Do People Grow on Family Trees? *(cont.)*

- Students can imagine what the first few days may have been like as a new immigrant in the United States. To record the details, have them write three diary entries from the immigrant's point of view.

- Invite someone who actually came to the United States through Ellis Island to speak to the class. Prepare students by having them discuss possible questions in advance.

(Chapter 5)

- Using the list of genealogical jewels found on page 77 of *Do People Grow on Family Trees?*, have students find out if they might have access to any of the means suggested to aid in their search for information.

- Have students begin collecting family photos. These photos should be accompanied by a short narrative describing the people in each photo and the place where each photo was taken.

- Oral history is very important. Before writing tools existed, stories were passed down from generation to generation by simply telling them. Have students ask their closest relatives for a favorite story. Encourage them to tape record the story or take notes. Then they can write the story using the special bordered paper on page 13. These family stories can be collected for the family history book.

- Explain to students that someday, in the future, it may interest someone to know what life was like in the 1990's. Have students take notes for one week regarding the types of activities they participate in, the types of stories highlighted in the news, the type of music that is popular, etc. Then have them write a narrative titled, "A Week in the Life of____." It is also important to have students include the dates in which the information was recorded. They may also wish to include documentation such as newspaper clippings, record labels, etc.

(Chapters 6-7)

- Read "Coming to America: My Grandmother's Story" to the class. The story is located on page 14. You may ask students to respond either verbally or in writing to this piece.

- The immigrants brought their cultural foods to America. Have students make foods representative of their own culture. Then have a "cultural food fair" celebration day.

Do People Grow on Family Trees? *(cont.)*

- Have students become detectives and try to find out where their last name came from. Several options are listed on page 108 of *Do People Grow on Family Trees?*. These include: patronymics, place names, occupational names, and nicknames. Then ask students if they had to adopt a new last name, what would it be and why would they choose it.

(Chapters 8-9)

- The U.S. Government adopted the "soundex" system to help with last names that can be spelled many different ways. Have students soundex their names by following the directions on page 139 of *Do People Grow on Family Trees?*.
- Some local libraries house genealogical records. Have students research to find out if any library in their area houses genealogical records.
- Many immigrants became American citizens. In order to do this they needed to fill out immigration papers. Challenge students to find out what is involved in becoming a citizen today.

(Chapter 10)

- Using all the information they have obtained throughout this unit, students can create a family history book. *Do People Grow on Family Trees?* suggests that students include the following in their family book:

  An introduction

  History of the family from past to present

  Description of how the family came to America

  A family tree

  Any photographs, documents, etc.

  An index of names

  A family roster

Students may use the cover design located on page 15 for their family history book, or they can design one of their own.

The Great Melting Pot

On the melting pot pattern below, write the name of your first family member to arrive in America, the date he/she arrived, and where he/she came from.

Interview Sheet

Use this interview sheet when interviewing close members of your family. You may wish to tape record the interviews if you have access to a tape recorder. All interview notes should be kept in your notebook or binder.

What is your full name? _____

Were you named after anyone? _____

When were you born? _____

Where were you born? _____

If you weren't born in the United States, when did you arrive here? _____

_____

What are your parents' names? _____

What are the names of your brothers and/or sisters? _____

_____

What countries/states/cities did you grow up in? _____

What do you remember about the house you lived in? _____

_____

_____

What do you remember most about your childhood? _____

_____

_____

_____

_____

List at least three more questions you would like to ask during the interview.

_____

_____

_____

_____

_____

Your Personal History

Answer the questions below about your own personal history. You may not know as much about yourself as you think you do!

1. What is your full name? _____

2. Were you named after anyone? _____

3. When were you born? _____

4. Where were you born? _____

5. How much did you weigh at birth? _____

6. How tall were you at birth? _____

7. What are your parents' full names? _____

    _____

8. When and where were they born? _____

9. Where do you live now? _____

10. Where else have you lived? _____

    _____

    _____

11. What are the names of your brothers and/or sisters? _____

    _____

12. When and where were they born? _____

    _____

13. What are the full names of your grandparents on both sides of your family?

    _____

    _____

Your Personal History *(cont.)*

14. What are your favorite things to do? _____

_____

15. What are your favorite foods? _____

_____

16. Are you on any teams? _____

17. What are your favorite subjects in school? _____

_____

18. What type of job would you like to have as an adult? _____

_____

19. List the names of several of your friends. _____

_____

20. Describe your most memorable moment. _____

_____

_____

21. Describe your most embarrassing moment. _____

_____

_____

22. What two famous people would you most like to meet and why?

_____

23. What other information would you like future generations to know about you?

_____

_____

Preserving the Oral Tradition

Using the taped recording of the story told to you by a relative, or your own detailed notes, retell the family story using the special bordered paper below. These stories will be used in compiling your family history book.

Coming to America: My Grandmother's Story

Read this true story of an Italian immigrant with your class. Then have students respond to it either verbally or in writing.

In 1926, I came to America and settled in Chicago, Illinois. My dad and part of my family were already here and working in factories to send for the rest of us — my mom, my youngest brother, and me.

We left my oldest brother behind because he was married and over the age of 18, which at the time was the law. Our leaving him behind put a very sad feeling on all of us, especially my delicate mom. We boarded the train in Catonia, Sicily to take us to the port in Palermo in order to leave Italy and embark on the ship that was going to America. It was called *Providence*.

After four days my younger brother and I were already getting used to the rocky trip and being seasick. By then, we were roaming around from one end of the ship to the other. We never saw my mom until it was time to eat. In just eight days we would arrive in Newark, New Jersey. Of course, before we went to Newark, we had to stop at the battery house called Ellis Island.

At Ellis Island we were herded around like cattle. We were physically checked for disease and tuberculosis. My mom was taken aside because she had an eye infection. She was put in the hospital across from our building which was separated by the Hudson River. My dad watched us to make sure we were safe.

The time away from my mom was unhappy. On top of this, our food was very limited. I did, however, look forward to the red shiny apples we got at every meal.

What I remember most from this trip was seeing the Statue of Liberty for the first time. It was looking at me saying, "Welcome to the free land of America." Thank God I am here!

My Family History Book

Use this cover for your own personal family history book. Make it colorful and inviting to read!

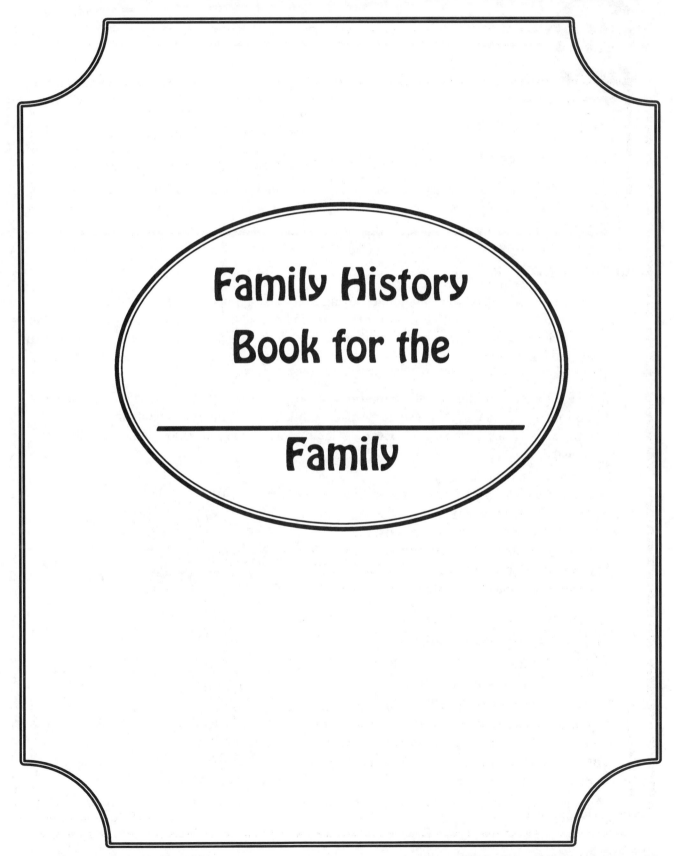

Family History
Book for the

_____
Family

My Backyard History Book

Author: David Weitzman

Illustrator: James Robertson

Publisher: Little, Brown and Company, Boston, 1975. 125 pages

Summary: This book provides simple ideas for how children can go about obtaining information about their family's history. Sections include: Getting a Line of Your Past, Hand-Me-Down History, History in the Yellow Pages, and History in a Small Way. This book is part of the popular Brown Paper School Series.

Learning Activities:

- Students may think they know about their own family history, but they may not really know that much beyond the superficial. Encourage them to find out how much they know about their family by taking the personal history test located on pages 16-17 of *My Backyard History Book*. Then discuss the results of the test with the students. Were they surprised at how much or little they knew?

- Challenge students to find out where their last name came from. Is it a patronym, nickname, occupation, or birthplace? Have students make a time line of important events in their lives by using the activity sheet on page 19. Then ask them to write about the most important of all the events listed.

- *My Backyard History Book* mentions making a birthday time capsule. Have students make a classroom time capsule. Determine the size of the box and then limit items to that size. Photographs or drawings of larger items can be included, as well as written descriptions. Students should each nominate items that they think would appropriately represent the time they spent in the class. Then, the class can vote and decide what will be placed in the classroom capsule.

- Make a generation bulletin board for the classroom. Have students bring in old family photos and documents. Along with each, they should write a brief note, perhaps on an index card, to go along with what they brought in. You can create a collage effect by grouping the materials together or give each student a special spot for his/her personal display.

- Using the United States map located in the appendix of this book, have students mark the areas where they have relatives living.

My Backyard History Book (cont.)

- Have students interview close relatives to uncover more about their family history. The questions on page 33 of *My Backyard History Book* provide a good starting place. You can also have the class brainstorm other questions to add to the list. Or they can use the interview sheets located on pages 10, 11, and 12 of this book.

- Have students make a pictorial family tree. To do this they will need to have pictures of themselves, parents, and grandparents. They can use the outline provided on page 20 of this book.

- A kinship chart is described on pages 38-39 of *My Backyard History Book*. Challenge students to make their own kinship chart using the few, simple symbols described on those pages.

- Have students collect old recipes that have been in their families for generations. Then have students neatly print a recipe on the recipe card on page 21 of this book. These recipe cards can then be cut out and placed in a class cultural cookbook. Perhaps the cookbook could be sold as a fund raiser for the school or classroom.

- Music has changed through the generations. Have students bring in any records they or their parents have from the 40's, 50's, 60's, 70's, 80's, and 90's. Then, have students compare the music styles across generations using the activity sheet on page 22.

- Challenge students to begin a family archive of photos, documents, and stories. In order to begin gathering information from relatives, have students draft a letter describing their project and needs that can be sent to relatives from whom they want assistance. Once they have collected some artifacts, they can begin putting them into a family archive book. A sample cover sheet can be found on page 23 of this book.

- As a class, brainstorm different family traditions across cultures. On the board make a comparison chart, letting students list the similarities found in various traditions.

- Have students do a retrospective project wherein they research the way a certain object or place has changed through time. Some wonderful project suggestions can be found on page 62 of *My Backyard History Book*. Then, have students write a brief report of their findings.

My Backyard History Book *(cont.)*

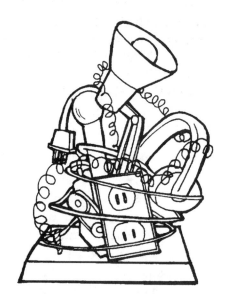

- When we don't know what to call something, it is often referred to as a "thingamajig." Have students bring something from home or a picture of something difficult to identify. Then have students try to guess what it is. The winner is the person who stumps the class with his or her mystery thingamajig.

- Challenge students to find the origin of three street names in their community. In other words, they'll discover whether streets are named after a famous person, place, or event. Suggest they speak to long-time residents of the community, realtors, and city officials to locate the origin.

- A long time ago, last names were often used to identify someone's occupation, place of residence, or nickname. Have students look in the phone book to find five names that could identify either someone's occupation, place of residence, or nickname.

- Neighborhoods change drastically over time. Have the class brainstorm questions they would want to ask their neighbors to find out what their neighborhood was like some time ago. Then have students interview at least two neighbors for their perspectives on the changes. If students live in a new neighborhood, have them find out what it looked liked before anything was built.

- To illustrate the answers uncovered from the neighbor interviews, have students ask the neighbors if they have any old photos of the city, or students can be encouraged to go to the local city council and ask for any brochures on the city that might contain old photos.

- Some local libraries have a special section for local history. Have students visit local libraries to find out if such resources exist in their community. Then, ask students to find three bits of information about the history of their city to share with the rest of the class.

- To preserve engravings and special designs, historians often use rubbings of the object. *My Backyard History Book* offers directions on how to do rubbings as well as provides suggestions for items in the neighborhood of which students might want to have a rubbing. Assign students to collect at least one rubbing.

- Have students tour the neighborhood in search of an old building or house. Then have them make as detailed a sketch of the place as possible. Have students keep this sketch.

- Using the sketch from the previous activity, students can recreate the building by using the suggestions on pages 120-121 of *My Backyard History Book*. When their building is complete, it can be displayed along side the drawing the student made.

Your Time Line

Below is a time line for you to complete, noting the most important events in your life. Once you have completed the time line, choose one event that is most meaningful to you and write a short narrative about the event and why it is important to you.

Year you were born

Current Year

A Special Family Tree

Using the outline below, make a pictorial family tree. Your picture will be at the base of the tree followed by that of your parents and grandparents.

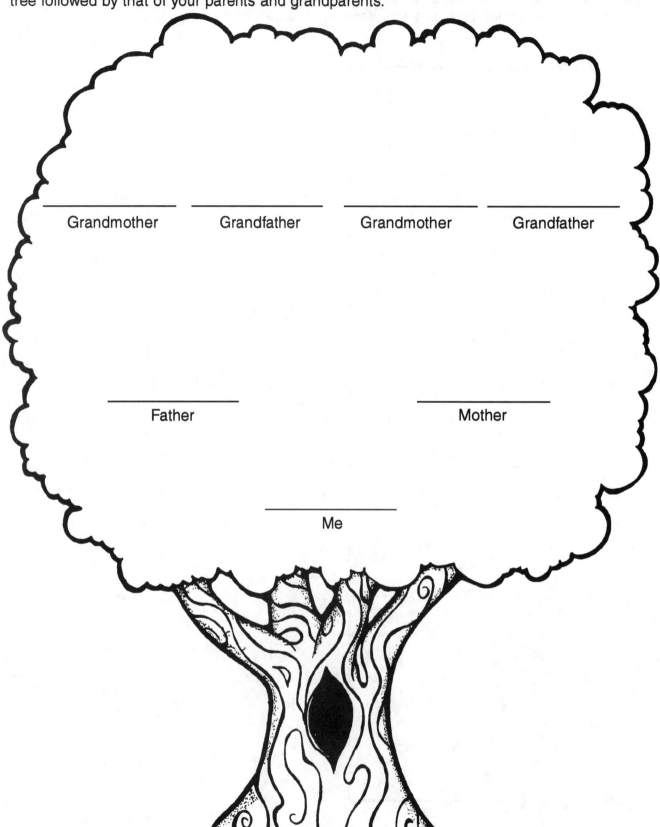

Grandmother   Grandfather   Grandmother   Grandfather

Father   Mother

Me

Cultural Cookbook

Using the recipe card pattern below, neatly copy the family recipe you have obtained. These recipes will be collected and placed in a Classroom Cultural Cookbook for everyone to enjoy!

Ingredients:

_____

_____

_____

_____

_____

_____

Directions:

_____

_____

_____

_____

_____

_____

Waltz, Rock, or Rap?

Music styles have changed considerably across the generations. Listen to music from the 40's, 50's, 60's, 70's, 80's, and 90's. Then choose music from just three periods to compare using the questions below.

1. List some of the lyrics from the three songs you are comparing.

   _____

   _____

   _____

2. How do the lyrics of the three types of music differ? _____

   _____

   _____

   _____

3. Is the beat different in each of the types of music? How is it different? _____

   _____

   _____

   _____

4. Consider the band names from the three selections you chose. How have names changed through the years? _____

   _____

   _____

5. Could you dance the same way to all three types of music? What dance style is appropriate for each of your selections? _____

   _____

   _____

   _____

My Family Archive

After you have sent your letter to relatives asking them for old photos and documents, hopefully you will begin receiving information that you will want to put in your family archive. Use the pattern below to create a cover sheet for the family archive book you will be working on throughout this unit.

Personal History

Baseball in April and Other Stories

Author: Gary Soto

Publisher: Harcourt, Brace and Jovanovich, San Diego, 1990.
134 pages

Summary: This book consists of vignettes that describe the childhood of Gary Soto and the people he lived with, went to school with, and knew in his neighborhood. Spanish words are woven into the text for effect. A glossary of the Spanish terms is provided in the book.

Learning Activities:

"Broken Chain"

- Prince was a popular rock star at the time *Baseball in April* was written. Alfonso wanted to look like Prince. Have students write about a current popular celebrity they would like to look like. Also have them write about why they want to look like that celebrity.

"Baseball in April"

- Have students write about a time they wanted to be part of a sports team or other group that required a try out or audition. Have them describe what the experience was like. Also, have them offer suggestions for novices on how to overcome being so nervous during try outs.

- Have students in small groups discuss why they think Michael did not make the baseball team.

- Let your children play a game of softball or tennis baseball where they substitute a tennis ball and racquet for a baseball and bat.

"Two Dreamers"

- Have students locate Fresno on a California map.

- Give students an opportunity to eat "frijoles" or beans like the children in the story do. Canned "frijoles" are available in the international food section of many supermarkets.

- Hector's grandfather could not communicate with the English-speaking real estate agent. Have students imagine that the grandfather had been able to negotiate with the real estate agent. Then have them write the negotiation conversation they think may have take place between the two characters.

* **Fresno**

- Hector's grandfather is interested in buying a house. Have children find out the price of homes in their neighborhoods. Bring in the real estate section of the classified ads and share some of the information with the children. Compare the price of homes with those that the grandfather was looking into.

Baseball in April and Other Stories (cont.)

"Barbie"

- Have students describe a special toy of their own. Ask them to include in their description who gave them the toy and why it is so special.

"The No-Guitar Blues"

- Fausto liked the band Los Lobos. Have students work in small groups to come up with a list of the current ten most popular musical groups.

"Seventh Grade"

- Have students write a story about one of their first days at school at any grade level.

"Mother and Daughter"

- Have students draw what Yollie looked like in her special dress before she left for the dance. Then have them draw a picture of Yollie after the dance.
- Have students discuss who they think felt worse about the dress mishap, Yollie or her mother.

"Karate Kid"

- Allow all students to watch the video of *Karate Kid.*
- Have students consider how Gilbert could have better handled the situation with the bully. Then have them write a letter of advice to Gilbert.

"La Bamba"

- Allow students to organize and perform a classroom talent show.

"The Marble Champ"

- Have students make up a marble game of their own.

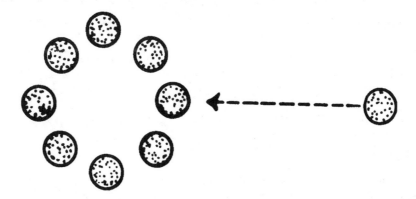

"Growing Up"

- Have students discuss whether or not they think Maria should have to go on vacation with her family.
- Now that students have completed the book, have them write a short vignette about themselves or one of their friends.

Personal History Bibliography

Beller, Susan Provost. *Roots for Kids: A Genealogy Guide for Young People.* (Betterway Publications, 1989)

Boyer, Carl. *How to Publish and Market Your Family History.* (Boyer Publisher, 1982)

Cosgriff, John & Carolyn Cosgriff. *Climb it Right: A High-Tech Genealogy Primer.* (Heritage Press, 1986)

Crandall, Ralph. *Shaking Your Family Tree: A Basic Guide to Tracing Your Family's Genealogy.* (Yankee, 1986)

Croom, Emily Anne. *Unpuzzling Your Past: A Basic Guide to Genealogy.* (Betterway Publications, 1989)

Doane, Gilbert H. & James B. Bell. *Searching for Your Ancestors: The How and Why of Genealogy.* (University of Minnesota Press, 1980)

Fletcher, William. *Recording Your Family History.* (Dodd, Mead, 1986)

Helmbold, F. Wilbur. *Tracing Your Ancestry: A Step-by-Step Guide to Researching Your Family History.* (Sepher-Hermon Press, 1979)

Henriod, Lorraine. *Ancestor Hunting.* (Simon & Schuster, 1979)

Hilton, Suzanne. *Who do You Think You Are? Digging for Your Family Roots.* (Westminster Press, 1976)

Lichtman, Allan. *Your Family History: How to Use Oral History, Family Archives, & Public Documents to Discover Your Heritage.* (Vintage Books, 1978)

Pellowski, Anne. *The Family Storytelling Handbook: How to Use Stories, Anecdotes, Rhymes, Handkerchiefs, Paper and Other Objects to Enrich Your Family Traditions.* (Macmillan, 1987)

Perl, Lila. *The Great Ancestor Hunt: The Fun of Finding Out Who You Are.* (Houghton Mifflin, 1989)

I, Columbus

Editor: Peter and Connie Roop

Illustrator: Peter E. Hanson

Publisher: Walker and Company, New York, 1990. 55 pages

Summary: The authors have taken passages from Columbus' log to recreate the events of his voyage from 1492-1493.

Learning Activities:

- Using the maps on pages 29 and 30 have the students chart Columbus' course to the New World and then his voyage home again as you read his diary entries to the class.

- Have students draw a picture of a sailboat and label all its parts (e.g., the rudder, bow, stern, keel, mast, jibe, sail, and tiller). See the example.

- At one point in the voyage, Pinzon decided to sail the *Pinta* off on his own in order to find gold and reap the rewards for himself. Pinzon later begged Columbus for forgiveness and approval to rejoin his voyage. Have students present a mock trial in which Pinzon must go before the King and Queen to explain why he went off on his own and to ask for their forgiveness. Students can volunteer to play certain roles.

- When the crewmen saw a meteorite, they considered it a bad omen. Have students research other superstitions of the sea.

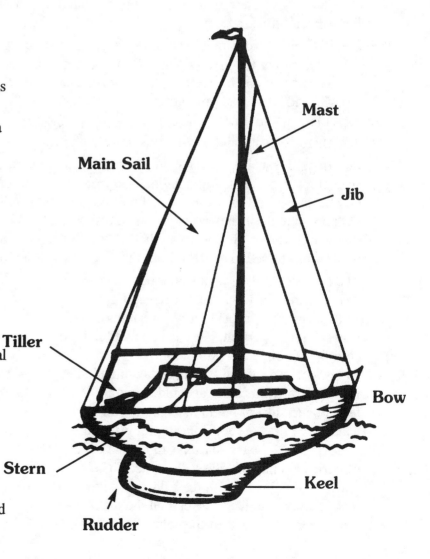

I, Columbus (cont.)

- Allow students to make their own sailboats using a small plastic bottle. The directions are simple enough!

  Materials: plastic bottle, sand, pencil, small piece of paper

  1. Lay the bottle sideways and make a hole large enough to insert a pencil. This will be the mast. Students can design a special flag to attach to the mast.

  2. Now, uncap the bottle and add enough sand to keep the bottle stable when placed in water. Replace the cap and shake the sand so it is evenly spread across the bottom of the bottle. The boat is now ready to sail!

- Columbus richly describes the island of Fernandina. Students can use watercolors to draw this rich and colorful landscape.

- Some of the natives Columbus met were using available gold to make jewelry. Allow students to make "macaroni jewelry." Using different types of macaroni, students can string it together to make necklaces and bracelets. Then, students can paint the jewelry with gold paint. For extra sparkle, add a touch of gold glitter.

- When Columbus reached Lisbon he decided to write to the King of Portugal to ask permission to land there. Have students write this letter to the King.

- Surprise students by making gold. In order to do this experiment you will need the following: several test tubes, potassium iodide, and lead nitrate (available through Carolina Supply 919-226-6000). In two test tubes, mix equal portions of the two chemicals. Cover the test tubes tightly with aluminum foil and ask several students to vigorously shake the tubes. While they are doing this, ask the other students to predict what will happen when the foil is removed. The white powder has turned to gold!! (Hint: the finer the powder, the better the color change)

- The crewmen sailing with Columbus were deathly afraid of volcanoes. You can let students make a volcano with just baking soda, water, liquid detergent, citric acid, and blue food coloring for effect. It's simple! Mix one tablespoon (15 mL) of baking soda with a half-full glass of warm water and add about a teaspoon (5 mL) of liquid detergent. You may add a few drops of food coloring for effect if you wish. Stir. Now, sprinkle about one capful of citric acid into the glass all at once. The citric acid will react with the baking soda to make carbon dioxide. The carbon dioxide will blow bubbles because of the detergent. Voila!

Columbus' Voyage to the New World

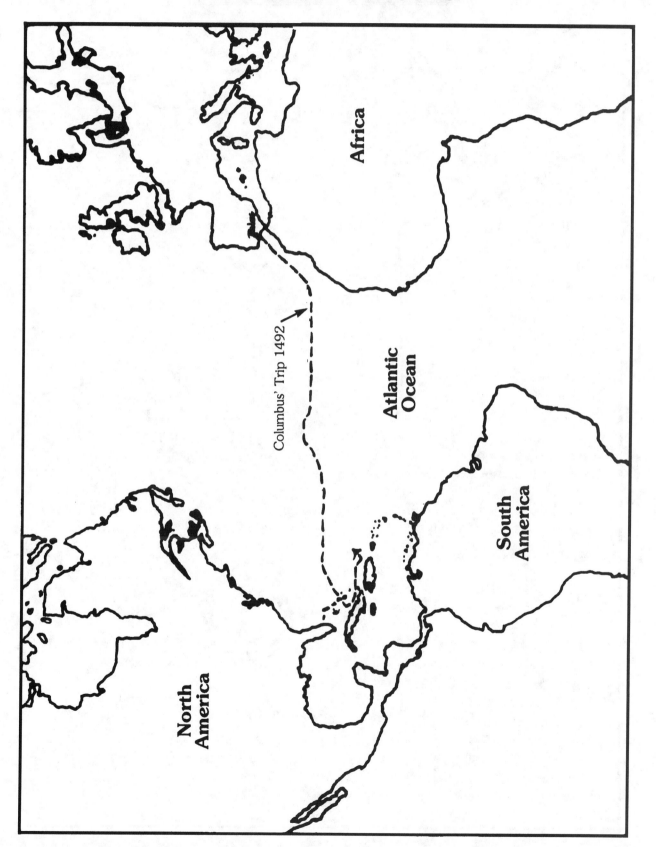

Columbus' Voyage Home

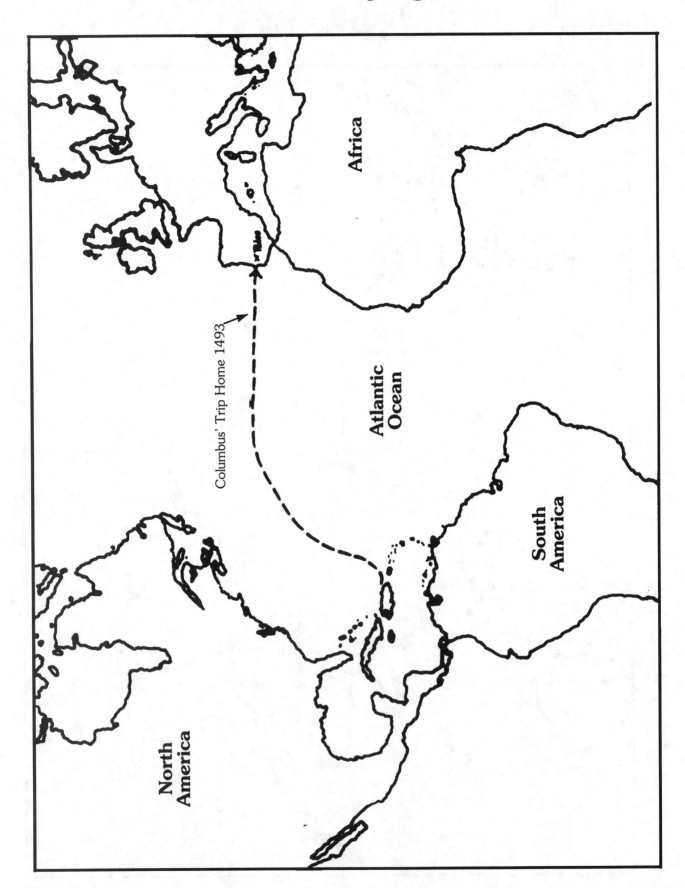

Pedro's Journal

Author: Pam Conrad

Illustrator: Peter Koeppen

Publisher: Boyd Mills Press, Pennsylvania, 1991. 96 pages

Summary: This detailed narrative chronicles Columbus' voyage as seen through the eyes of a cabin boy, Pedro de Salcedo. Pedro's journal spans the time period of August 3, 1492–February 14, 1493.

Learning Activities:

- The crewmen on the voyage often spoke of sea monsters. Pedro was afraid of the stories. Have children write and illustrate their own sea monster stories.

- Columbus' voyage rests on the accuracy of his compass. Students can make a simple compass by following these directions.

   Materials: a regular compass to use for comparison, a cork, bar magnet, sewing needle, and a small bowl for water

   1. Cut off a piece of cork approximately ³/₄ of an inch (1.9 cm). Then, cut a straight groove across the cork to rest the needle on.

   2. Rub one end of the needle about 30 times in the same direction on a magnet. Then place the needle on the cork. Place the cork in a shallow bowl of water and students will be amazed to watch the needle point to the north!

- The crewmen continue to see mirages because they are so desperate to find land. Students may have seen mirages of water before; they are fairly common. Have students research what a mirage is and how it happens.

- Pedro's first time in water is an exciting experience. Have students write a story describing their first experience in the water or ocean.

- Have students research the purpose for the different types of sails used on the three ships. The following types of sails were mentioned: main topsail, fore course, spritsail, lateen mizzen, and bona venture mizzen.

Pedro's Journal *(cont.)*

- If you had your class read *I, Columbus* from the previous assignment, ask them to compare and contrast that journal to *Pedro's Journal*. Students can use the following format to help organize their thoughts.

The voyage through Pedro's eyes	The voyage through Columbus' eyes
Similarities	**Differences**

- On several occasions Pedro describes the beauty of the sea and being able to see the creatures in the ocean. Have students do a crayon resist of an ocean scene. Follow the directions below.

    Materials: fluorescent crayons work best, but any crayons will work; construction paper; blue watercolor paints

    1. Using the crayons, draw a detailed picture of ocean creatures.
    2. Using blue watercolors, paint over the entire picture. The paint resists covering the crayon. This makes a colorful art project good for bulletin board display.

- Have students in groups discuss whether or not they think Columbus treated the natives he met with respect.

- Pedro was very excited to be reunited with his mother. Have students in small groups write the reunion scene between Pedro and his mother. Then have student volunteers perform the scene.

- Ask students to imagine that Columbus had asked Pedro to go with him on his next voyage. Then, have them pretend they are Pedro and write a letter to Columbus either accepting the offer or rejecting it.

Christopher Columbus: A Great Explorer

Author and Illustrator: Carol Greene

Publisher: Childrens Press, Chicago, 1989. 45 pages

Summary: This book is a biography of the amazing life of explorer Christopher Columbus. It acknowledges that while Columbus was a great explorer, he was not the first to discover America because people already lived here.

Learning Activities:

- Have students locate Columbus' home town of Genoa, Italy, on a map in the classroom or the world map on page 144.

- Columbus and others described what they thought was the lush land and wealth of the Indies. Using the descriptions in the story, have students draw what Columbus thought the Indies looked like.

- On page 16 of *Christopher Columbus* are two different pictures of Columbus saying good-bye to Queen Isabella and sailing off to the New World. Have students compare how the pictures are alike and how they are different.

- Using the activity sheet on page 34, have students analyze Columbus' personality with the character map.

- Challenge students to find out about sea cows. Do they still exist? In what oceans do they live? How big are they?

- Bobadilla was sent by the King and Queen to check on Columbus when he was in Hispaniola. Have students write a letter from Bobadilla to the King and Queen describing what he saw and what he recommends as the punishment for Christopher Columbus.

- When Columbus returned to Spain, he had to answer to the King and Queen about what went on in Hispaniola. Have students write a scene between Columbus, the Queen, and the King as Columbus answers Bobadilla's allegations and explains his own actions.

- Choose several students to serve on a panel to determine what, if any, punishment Columbus should receive based on what he did to the Indians and natives.

Columbus, What a Character!

Using the character map below, consider the type of person Columbus was. In the center of the map is the person's name, Christopher Columbus. From that square are four attached circles. In these circles, list four of the most prominent characteristics of Columbus' personality. Then, for each aspect of his personality, use specific examples from the book to support your answer. Write them on the lines attached to the circles.

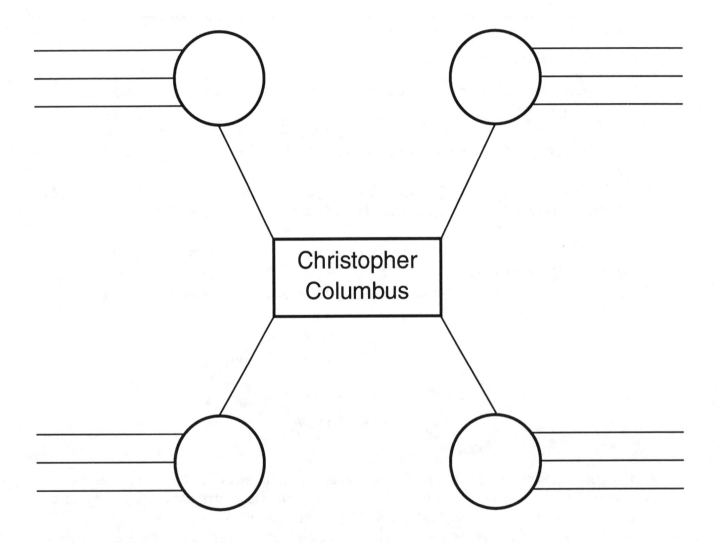

Bibliography

Adler, D. A. *Picture Book of Christopher Columbus.* (Holiday House, 1991)

Benchley, N. *Beyond the Mist.* (Harper, 1975)

Ceserani, G. P. *Christopher Columbus.* (Random, 1979)

Dagliesch, Alice. *America Begins: The Story of the Finding of the New World.* (Scribner, 1958)

D'Aulaire, Ingri, and Edgar P. D'Aulaire. *Columbus.* (Doubleday, 1955)

Fritz, Jean. *Brendan the Navigator.* (Coward, 1979)

Fritz, Jean. *Where Do You Think You're Going Christopher Columbus?* (Putnam, 1980)

Irwin, C. *Strange Footprints on the Land: Vikings in America.* (Harper, 1980)

Kurtz, H. I. *Captain John Smith.* (Watts, 1976)

Levinson, Nancy Smiler. *Christopher Columbus: Voyager to the Unknown.* (Lodestar, 1990)

Maestro, B., and G. Maestro. *The Discovery of the Americas.* (Lothrop, 1991)

Matthews, Rupert. *The Voyage of Columbus.* (Bookwright, 1989)

Melzter, M. *Christopher Columbus and the World Around Him.* (Watts, 1990)

Pelta, K. *Discovering Christopher Columbus: How History is Invented.* (Lerner, 1991)

Soule, Gardner. *Christopher Columbus on the Great Sea of Darkness.* (Watts, 1988)

Weil, L. I. *Christopher Columbus.* (Atheneum, 1983)

Yolen, Jane. *Encounter.* (Harcourt, 1992)

A Williamsburg Household

Author: Joan Anderson

Photographer: George Ancona

Publisher: Clarion Books, New York, 1988. 45 pages

Summary: This book provides a pictorial look at colonial life in Williamsburg, Virginia in the eighteenth-century.

Learning Activities:

- Have students define words no longer commonly used, such as rations, gentry, milliner, apothecary, and livery.
- Compare the lives of slaves and their owners by having students complete a contrast chart like the example below. Then have students write about one or two of the differences that really struck them personally.

Contrast Chart

A Day in the Life of a Slave	A Day in the Life of an Owner
Worked from sun up to sun down.	Everything was done for them.

- Have students predict what is going to become of Aberdeen.
- The slaves enjoyed telling stories to their families. Your students can each choose an African-American story to tell the class from the book *Many Thousand Gone: African Americans from Slavery to Freedom* by Virginia Hamilton (Alfred A. Knopf, 1993).
- In the book, Mrs. Moody likes to eat apple tarts and drink tea. Students can make apple turnovers using a very simple recipe found in *The Little House Cookbook* by Barbara M. Walker (HarperCollins, 1979). To make this colonial snack complete, have students brew some tea.
- Colonial life is certainly much different than modern life. Have students compare these two unique ways of life using the chart on page 37.

Life: Then and Now

Using the chart below, compare colonial life to modern day life. Consider what you read about Mr. and Mrs. Moody and their daughter Hannah when you complete the colonial life portion of the chart. Use your own experience to complete the modern day portion of the chart. When you have completed the chart, answer the questions that follow on a separate piece of paper.

	Colonial Life	**Modern Life**
Work		
Dress		
Chores		
Recreation		
Transportation		
Responsibility		

1. What do you think is the most dramatic change that has taken place?

2. If you suddenly were transported back to the colonial period, what would be the most difficult change for you?

The Pilgrims of Plimouth

Author and Illustrator: Marcia Sewall

Publisher: Atheneum, New York, 1986. 46 pages

Summary: This book provides a rich description of Pilgrim life with an in-depth comparison of differences in chores for men, women, and children. The story takes place in September, 1620.

Learning Activities:

- The Pilgrims had to develop their own laws of behavior. This was no easy task. To enable students to experience the difficulty in establishing rules/laws of behavior, have them determine a set of rules and consequences for the classroom. Ask students to establish the rules they feel are appropriate. Then have them meet in small groups to make the final selection of rules and consequences for the class.

- Corn seed is discussed in the story. Have students make cornbread, a popular colonial treat. A box mix can be purchased, or students can make the cornbread from scratch using the recipe below. Other cornbread recipes can be found in *The Little House Cookbook* by Barbara M. Walker (HarperCollins, 1979).

Cornbread

Ingredients:

³/₄ cup (177 mL) sifted all purpose flour

2 ¹/₂ teaspoons (12.5 mL) double-acting baking powder

1 ¹/₂ tablespoons (22.5 mL) sugar

³/₄ teaspoon (3.75 mL) salt

1 ¹/₄ cups (300 mL) yellow stone-ground cornmeal

1 egg

2 tablespoons (30 mL) butter

1 cup (236 mL) milk

Directions: Preheat oven to 425 degrees F (218 C°). Grease a 9" x 9" (23 cm x 23 cm) pan or a muffin pan. Sift flour, baking powder, sugar, and salt into a bowl. Add cornmeal. In a separate bowl, beat one egg, butter, and milk. Combine all and mix together. Bake about 15 minutes.

Makes about 15 muffins.

- At one point the pilgrims had the opportunity to go back to England. Discuss with students if they would have chosen to stay or return to England.

The Pilgrims of Plimouth (cont.)

- In this story, the women use trees and other plants as medicine. Have students research herbal medicine. Ask them to find out which herbs are considered to have healing abilities. You may also ask what they think of herbal medicine and whether or not it really works.

- The book describes in detail the chores of the men, women, and children pilgrims. Have students compare and contrast the responsibilities of these three groups of people by completing the Venn diagram on page 40. Then, students can analyze the information by answering the questions also included on the activity page.

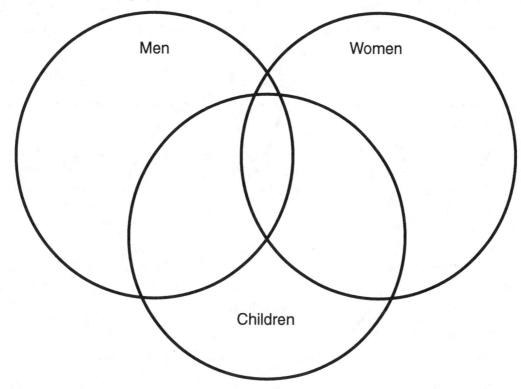

Men

Women

Children

- On page 21 in the book is a picture of a Pilgrim house. Have students make a model of a Pilgrim house using craft sticks and any other materials that are available.

- The Pilgrims established a peace treaty with the Native Americans. Have students work in small groups to draft what they think this peace treaty said. Then, students should be encouraged to share their treaties with the rest of the class.

- The Pilgrims planted many different types of herbs such as violet leaves, red sage, mint, and rosemary. Herbs are fairly easy to grow. Have students plant different herbs and chart their growth using the activity sheet on page 41.

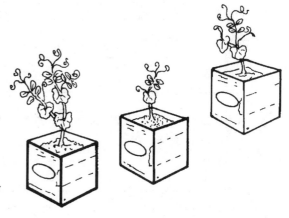

- The children enjoyed playing many different games. Some of the games your students are probably familiar with are: hide and seek and tug of war. Others they may not be familiar with are: stool ball or pitch the bar. Encourage students to learn to play all these games and then have an afternoon of fun outside!

It's Off to Work We Go!

The book describes in detail the chores and responsibilities for men, women, and children. Using the Venn diagram below, note the similarities and differences in responsibilities between the three groups. Then, analyze the information by answering the questions that follow.

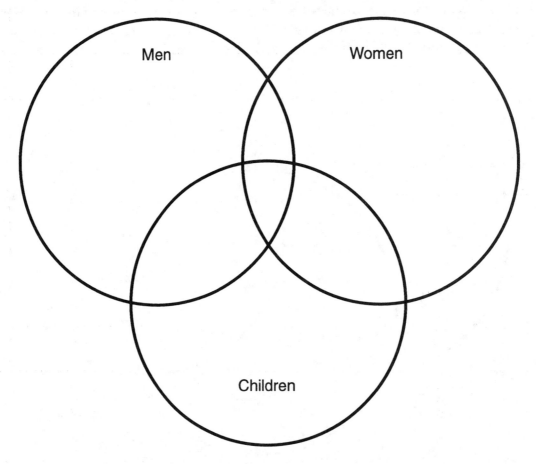

1. Is there an even distribution of the work? _____

   _____

   _____

2. Do the responsibilities follow the typical gender roles of the past? _____

   _____

   _____

3. If these responsibilities were to be divided between a family today, how would they be the same or different? _____

   _____

   _____

See How We Grow

Select an herb mentioned in the book to grow and chart. Some of the herbs mentioned include: violet leaves, red sage, mint, and rosemary. Plant your selected herb and then chart its growth using the graph below.

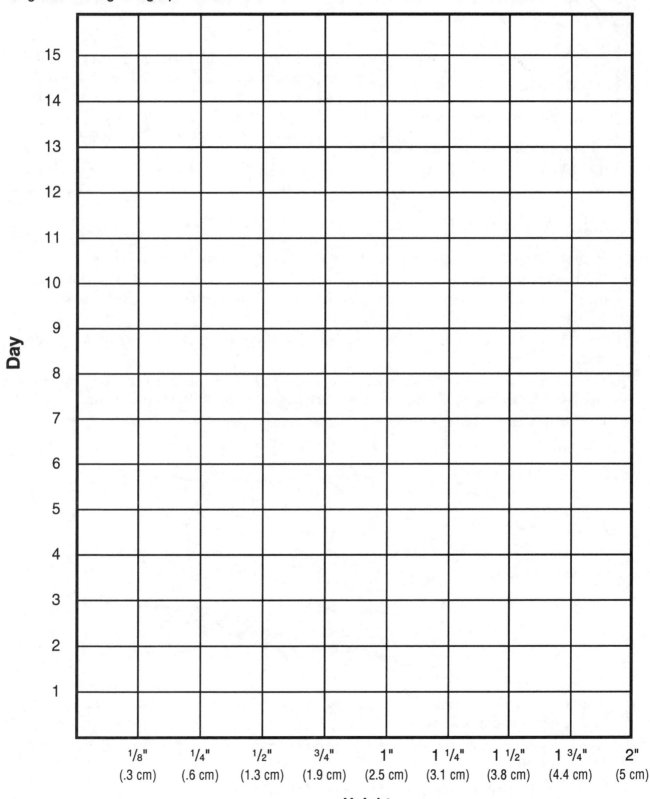

Height

Sarah Morton's Day: A Day in the Life of a Pilgrim Girl

Author: Kate Waters

Photographs: Russ Kendall

Publisher: Scholastic, New York, 1989. 31 pages

Summary: This book provides a pictorial description of the life of a Pilgrim girl in 1627. The full color photographs were taken at Plymouth Plantation, a living history museum in Plymouth, Massachusetts.

Learning Activities:

- Have students make a Pilgrim word dictionary using the terms explained in the book.

- The book begins with three riddles. Have students find riddle books and select two or three of their favorite riddles. Then have them copy their riddles onto the form on page 43. These can be collected to make a class riddle book for everyone to enjoy.

- Have students make a replica of the plantation Sarah lived on using sticks, toothpicks, and craft sticks.

- Have students write a speech denouncing the use of the "rod" as punishment. You may wish to discuss with them their feelings about Sarah getting the rod for speaking out of turn.

- Have students make Indian corn bread using the recipe in *Sarah Morton's Day* on page 14.

- Allow students to write a fancy alphabet like the one Sarah used on colored paper using colored chalk.

- Marbles was a popular game during that time period. Allow students to make up some marble games to play during recess time.

- As an art project, allow students to make a puppet like the one shown on page 28 of *Sarah Morton's Day.*

- Have students discuss why Sarah has to stand when she eats.

Our Book of Riddles

Using the forms below, write out your special, favorite riddles. Then, cut out the forms. On the back of the forms write the answer to the riddle. You may wish to write the answer upside down so it can't be read through the paper.

The Courage of Sarah Noble

Author: Alice Dalgliesh

Illustrator: Leonard Weisgard

Publisher: Macmillan, New York, 1954. 54 pages

Summary: In 1707, Sarah Noble and her father, John, journey to Connecticut by themselves to build a house for the family. This true story of Sarah's journey is inspiring.

Learning Activities:

- Sarah's father chose her to go with him because she was a good cook. She satisfied him with her delicious bean porridge. A simple recipe for bean porridge can be found in *The Little House Cookbook* by Barbara M. Walker (HarperCollins, 1979). Challenge students to make this special dish.

- Discuss with students what it means to have courage. They can use the word web and basic questions on the activity sheet on page 45 to help them organize their ideas.

- Have students in small groups discuss why the Native American children might have been afraid of Sarah in their first encounter. As a class, brainstorm the significance of Sarah's cloak.

- During this time period, children played very simple games. For example, the hidden pebble game was popular. Children took off their shoes and hid a pebble in one; the other children had to guess which shoe the pebble was in. This might be a good rainy day game for your class or fun to play at recess time.

- Have students write a thank-you letter to Tall John from Sarah for caring for her while her father was away.

- Have students predict what Sarah's future holds for her.

- The young boys told Sarah scary stories of Native Americans. Sarah was also a good storyteller herself. Have students write a scary story of sleeping outside in the wilderness that Sarah can tell the boys to scare them.

Word Web

It was sometimes difficult for Sarah to be courageous as she faced sleeping in the wilderness, visiting strangers, and listening to scary stories about Native Americans. However, she always remembered her mother telling her to keep up her courage.

What does courage mean to you? Use the word web below to brainstorm all the ideas that come to your mind when you think of the word courage. Then, answer the questions that follow.

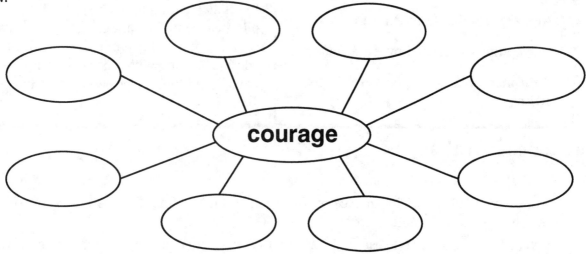

1. Choose three words that best describe what courage means to you. _____

   _____

2. Based on your definition, did Sarah have courage? _____

3. Think about a time when you had to show courage. Write a story describing the event.

   _____

   _____

   _____

   _____

   _____

   _____

   _____

   _____

   _____

   _____

   _____

Eating the Plates: A Pilgrim Book of Food and Manners

Author: Lucille Recht Penner

Illustrations: Selected by the Author

Publisher: Macmillan, New York, 1991. 107 pages

Summary: This is a charming book about the food, manners, and customs of the Pilgrims. Questions such as why the pilgrims ate in the dark on the *Mayflower* and why they planted fish in the corn fields are addressed along with other interesting facts. Favorite pilgrim recipes are also included.

Learning Activities:

(Chapters 1-4)

- The introduction begins with an excerpt from Samuel Francis Smith's *America*. Have students research *America* in its entirety.

- The food the pilgrims had to eat on the *Mayflower* was frequently very unappetizing. Have students make a "wacky" Mayflower menu using the activity sheet on page 48.

- John Carver was the first Governor to be elected by the Pilgrims. Have students write an acceptance speech for Mr. Carver.

- Hold a mock Thanksgiving feast with half the students being Pilgrims and the other half being Native American guests. Recipe suggestions are located in the back of *Eating the Plates*.

- As the colony became established, the need for workers increased: sawyers, tanners, and coopers were in high demand. Have students brainstorm a list of other occupations that would have been needed at that time.

(Chapters 5-10)

- It was said in the book that cooking was the most important activity in the Pilgrim household. Have students write a short story about the most important activity in their own home.

Eating the Plates *(cont.)*

- Have students write about what the most difficult change would be for them if they were suddenly transported back to the days of the Pilgrims.

- The Pilgrims made hasty pudding and the Native Americans made their own Indian pudding. Challenge students to make both and then have a taste test to see which they like better. A recipe for hasty pudding can be found on page 74 of this book. A recipe for Indian pudding can be found in *Eating the Plates* on page 95.

- The Pilgrims liked to drink apple cider. Obtain some apple cider from the store and then add some special ingredients. Heat the cider well and add a few cloves and a stick of cinnamon.

- The lives of the young Pilgrim children were very different from the lives of children now. Often they were left to guard the corn fields throughout the day. Also, children were allowed to drink beer. Have students compare their chores and privileges with the Pilgrim children.

- Pilgrims made their first spoons from shells. Obtain some shells from a local beach or a craft store as well as some craft sticks. Have students make their own special Pilgrim spoons.

- Compare manners and customs of Pilgrims with our customs today. Use the activity sheet on page 49 to assist students with the comparison.

- Challenge students to make a fancy Pilgrim feast by fixing some or all of the recipes in the back of *Eating the Plates*. Students can even make special costumes for the event. Native American vests can be made out of paper bags. Simply cut a hole in the top for the child's head and holes in the sides for arms. Then, have students decorate with crayons and beads if they are available. For the other students, pilgrim collars can be made by following the simple pattern below.

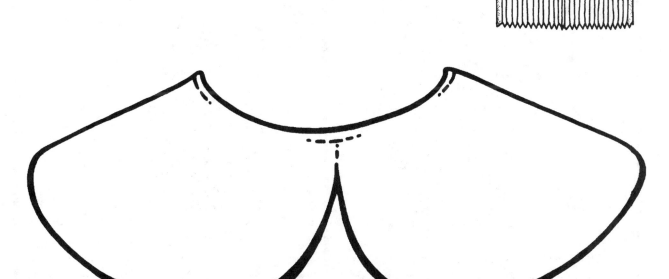

Mayflower Madness Menu

When the Pilgrims were on the *Mayflower* they had to eat some unappetizing things. Green, moldy cheese was one of them! Using the menu form below, create a wacky Mayflower Madness Menu. An appetizer example has been done for you. Remember, be creative!!

Menu

Appetizers
cracked Cockroaches

Main Dishes:

Menu

Side Dishes:

Desserts:

Are You Accustomed to Their Customs?

Listed below are the manners and customs of the Pilgrims for meal time. Compare those customs with those in your own home. How are they alike and/or different?

Pilgrim Customs	Your Customs
Use fingers instead of a fork to eat.	
Only take food given to you by your parents.	
Napkin tied around neck and hangs down to knees.	
Only the father sits in a chair; others sit on stools/children sometimes stand.	
Allowed to keep hat on during dinner.	
Never scratch at the table.	
Bones are piled neatly on the table.	
Everyone drinks from the same cup.	

Sign of the Beaver

Author: Elizabeth George Speare

Publisher: Houghton Mifflin, Boston, 1983. 135 pages

Summary: Matt and his father reluctantly leave the rest of their family behind to find a better home in Maine. After building a cabin, Matt's father leaves in order to bring the rest of the family to Maine. While his father is away, Matt befriends a Native American family who becomes his source of support during this difficult waiting period. However, when the Native American family decides to move north, Matt must decide whether to go with them or stay and wait for his family.

Learning Activities:

(Chapters 1-6)

- Before Matt's father left, he gave him a watch that was his grandfather's special possession. Have students brainstorm special possessions of theirs that they would leave for future generations. Then, have students write a short story about why the objects they chose were so meaningful.

- Have students discuss whether or not they think it was appropriate to leave 13 year-old Matt alone to fend for himself.

- Matt discovered he had a great deal of time on his hands without his father there to tell him what to do. Have students write a story about what they would do if they were left at home alone for an entire weekend.

- Matt regretted befriending Ben after he found out that Ben had stolen his gun. Have students in groups discuss how Matt could have avoided this unwanted stranger.

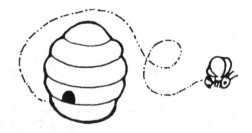

- Matt discovered that it is no easy task to get honey from bees. He really learned his lesson! Have students research how beekeepers manage to get the honey away from the bees.

- Attean left Matt some cornbread, much to his delight. Students may follow the recipe on page 38 or use boxed cornbread mix. It is easily obtained and simple to make. Have students make some cornbread for the class.

- As a class, have students discuss different methods for learning how to read. Ask them how they would go about teaching someone how to read. What suggestions would they give to Matt?

Sign of the Beaver *(cont.)*

- Have students complete a character study of Matt and Attean by completing the activity sheet on page 53.

(Chapters 7-13)

- For extra credit, have students read *Robinson Crusoe.*

- Matt tried to teach Attean how to read. Attean tried to teach Matt the ways of the land. Have students consider their strengths as teachers. This can be discussed in small groups.

- There were definite jobs for men and women during this time period. Things have changed since then, or have they? Divide the class into small groups of boys and girls and ask them to list what they consider men's work and what they consider women's work. Compare the responses of the boys and girls. Then discuss gender roles and stereotyping.

- Attean left little signs throughout the forest so he and Matt would be able to find their way back. Select several students to go to the playground and leave little clues to direct other students where to go. These should be small clues like Attean left. Then, challenge other students to follow the path.

- Being able to hit a target was very important for Matt to be able to eat. Have students practice hitting targets using tin cans of different sizes and small stones. Simply line up the tin cans and give students several small stones to try to hit the targets. Students can keep a record and possibly even graph their progress.

(Chapters 14-20)

- Girls did not do any of the hunting; it was left to men. Ask students if they think girls can hunt as well as men.

- In small groups, elect a student to tell the story of *Robinson Crusoe*, or any other adventure story they know, to the others as Attean may have told the story of Crusoe to his Native American family.

- Allow students to play the stone game as described in the story. Using six small stones, paint one side of each of the stones with red paint. Then students toss the stones, trying to get as many stones to land with the painted side up.

Sign of the Beaver *(cont.)*

- Attean explained to Matt that he had to get his manitou. This is a type of "coming of age" test. Ask students if they think there is a coming of age test for boys and girls now.

- Allow students to make Native American bean necklaces by following these easy directions.

Materials: bowl, water, food coloring, navy beans, needle, strong thread

1. Tint some water with food coloring. Soak dried beans in the water to soften and color them. This may take overnight.

2. Remove beans and string them using a needle and strong thread. Allow to dry. The beans may shrink as they dry.

(Chapters 21-25)

- Have students discuss if they think Matt should have taken the risk and stayed to wait for his father. What if he hadn't returned? What would have happened to Matt?

- Matt was looking forward to his mother's stewed cranberries. Students can easily make cranberry sauce using the recipe below.

Cranberry Sauce

Ingredients: 2 cups water (472 mL), 4 cups cranberries (1 lb.) (944 mL), 2 cups (472 mL) sugar

Directions: Wash cranberries. Place them in a saucepan and cover with 2 cups boiling water. When the water begins to boil again, cover and boil for 3-4 minutes. Put cranberries through a strainer, then back in the saucepan. Add sugar. Place over heat and bring to a boil. Remove from heat at once.

- Matt made his sister Sarah a corn husk doll as a present for when she reached the new house. Students can make a cornhusk doll. Directions appear on page 59.

- Have students write a conversation between Matt's parents discussing his relationship with the Native Americans while they were gone.

- Both Matt and Attean are very smart, but in different ways. Have students complete the literary and Life-Skills report cards for Matt and Attean on pages 54 and 55.

Character Study

In this activity you will study two characters, Matt and Attean. Use specific examples from the book whenever possible to support your answers.

Facts About Matt's Past and His Family	Matt's Personality Traits	Matt's Physical Characteristics

Facts About Attean's Past and His Family	Attean's Personality Traits	Attean's Physical Characteristics

Literary Report Cards

Complete these school-subjects report cards for Matt and Attean. Then complete the life-skills report cards on the following page. Be sure to give fair grades as well as meaningful comments.

Report Card for: Matt

Subject	Grade	Comments
Reading/Writing		
Science		
Math		
Social Studies		
Physical Education		

Report Card for: Attean

Subject	Grade	Comments
Reading/Writing		
Science		
Math		
Social Studies		
Physical Education		

Life-Skills Report Cards *(cont.)*

After completing the report cards for Matt and Attean, answer the questions at the bottom of the page.

Report Card for: Matt

Subject	Grade	Comments
Survival Skills		
Physical Science		
Sense of Direction		
Friendship		

Report Card for: Attean

Subject	Grade	Comments
Survival Skills		
Physical Science		
Sense of Direction		
Friendship		

1. What does "smart" mean to each of the boys? _____

_____

2. What does "smart" mean to you? _____

_____

Bibliography

Anderson, Joan. *A Williamsburg Household.* (Houghton & Mifflin, 1988)

Bains, Rae. *Pilgrims & Thanksgiving.* (Troll, 1985)

Barth, E. *Turkeys, Pilgrims and Indian Corn: The Story of Thanksgiving Symbols.* (Clarion, 1975)

Bulla, C. R. *A Lion to Guard Us.* (Crowell, 1981)

Bulla, C. R. *Charlie's House.* (Knopf, 1993)

Campbell, Elizabeth. *Jamestown: The Beginning.* (Little, Brown, 1974)

Clapp, Patricia. *Constance: A Story of Early Plymouth.* (Penguin, 1986)

Corwin, Judith. *Colonial American Crafts: The Home.* (Watts, 1989)

D'Amato J., and A. D'Amato. *Colonial Crafts for You to Make.* (Messner, 1975)

Edmonds, Walter. *Matchlock Gun.* (Troll, 1991)

Field, Rachael. *Calico Bush.* (Dell, 1988)

Fisher, Leonard Everett. *The Homemakers.* (Watts, 1973)

Fradin, Dennis. *New Hampshire Colony.* (Childrens, 1987)

Fritz, Jean. *Who's that Stepping on Plymouth Rock?* (Coward, 1973)

Hooks, William H. *Legend of the White Doe.* (Macmillan, 1988)

Hoople, C. G. *The Heritage Sampler: A Book of Colonial Arts and Crafts.* (Dial, 1975)

Kalman, Bobbie. *Colonial Life.* (Crabtree, 1992)

Kalman, Bobbie. *Colonial Town: Williamsburg.* (Crabtree, 1992)

Kurelek, William & Margaret Engelhart. *They Sought a New World: The Story of European Immigration to North America.* (Tundra, 1985)

Loeb, R. H. *Meet the Real Pilgrims: Everyday Life on a Plymouth Plantation.* (Doubleday, 1979)

Loeper, John. *Going to School in 1776.* (Atheneum, 1973)

Madison, Arnold. *How the Colonists Lived.* (McKay, 1980)

McGovern, Ann. *If You Lived in Colonial Times.* (Scholastic, 1969)

Milhouse, Nicholas and Margaret Bowman. *Blue Feather's Vision, the Dawn of Colonial America.* (Troll, 1982)

Penner, L. R. *The Colonial Cookbook.* (Hastings, 1976)

Perl, L. *Slumps, Grunts, and Snicker Doodles: What Colonial America Ate and Why.* (Clarion, 1975)

Sabin, Louis. *Colonial Life in America.* (Troll, 1985)

Sewall, Marcia. *Pilgrims of Plimoth.* (Macmillan, 1986)

Siegel, Beatrice. *Fur Trappers & Traders: The Indians, the Pilgrims, & the Beaver.* (Walker & Co., 1987)

Smith, C. (Ed). *The Explorers and Settlers: A Source Book on Colonial America.* (Millbrook, 1991)

Speare, Elizabeth. *The Witch of Blackbird Pond.* (Houghton Mifflin, 1958)

Tunis, Edwin. *Colonial Living.* (Crowell, 1976)

Pioneer Children of Appalachia

Author: Joan Anderson

Photographer: George Ancona

Publisher: Clarion Books, New York, 1986. 46 pages

Summary: This book chronicles the life of a family living in the Appalachian mountains in the spring.

Learning Activities:

- One of the jobs the children had to do was to make candles. Students can make their own candles following these simple directions. Note: Melting wax can be a dangerous activity. Supervise carefully.

Materials: tin cans, self-adhesive paper, permanent markers, heavy string, nails, old candle pieces or paraffin

1. Thoroughly clean an empty tin can. Decorate with markers. Use the self-adhesive paper to cover the can.

2. Next, cut a piece of heavy string slightly longer than the can. Tie the string to the center of a nail long enough to stretch across the top of the can. This string will become the candle wick.

3. Now melt some old candle pieces or paraffin in an old coffee can by placing the can in a saucepan containing a small amount of water and heating on medium temperature. With the nail and string in place, pour the hot wax into the can. When the wax has hardened, snip off the nail still attached to the wick. The candle is ready!

Pioneer Children of Appalachia *(cont.)*

- The children in the story were told tales of hardship by their grandmother. Have students interview their own grandparents or other adults to find out what life was like for them as a child. Then, have them choose one story to write and illustrate. Use the special bordered paper on page 60. These stories can be collected and compiled into a class book.

- Pioneer men and women had very traditional roles. The men were responsible for hunting the food and doing the heavy work, while the women kept house and cooked. In small groups, have students discuss the changing roles of men and women. How do gender roles today differ from the days of the pioneers?

- Have students write a diary entry from the point of view of either of the children describing what the winter is like.

- Your students can make a class quilt simply using construction paper. Cut out multicolored squares of construction paper, enough for each student to have one square. Then have students draw a design on their square that represents some aspect of pioneer life. When all students have completed their squares, they can be put together to make a colorful class quilt that can be displayed in the classroom.

- The pioneer children enjoyed eating gingerbread. Your students can make their own gingerbread by following the recipe below.

Gingerbread

Ingredients:
- ¹/₂ cup (120 mL) butter
- ¹/₂ cup (120 mL) sugar
- 1 egg
- 2 ¹/₂ cups (590 mL) sifted all purpose flour
- 1 ¹/₂ teaspoons (7.5 mL) baking soda
- 1 teaspoon (5 mL) cinnamon
- 1 teaspoon (5 mL) ginger
- ¹/₂ teaspoon (2.5 mL) salt
- ¹/₂ cup (120 mL) light molasses
- ¹/₂ cup (120 mL) honey
- 1 cup (250 mL) hot water

Directions: Preheat oven to 350 F degrees (177 C°). Melt the butter in a 9" x 9" x 2" (23.5 cm x 23.5 cm x 5 cm) pan and let cool. Into a bowl add and beat well sugar and egg. Sift flour, baking soda, cinnamon, ginger and salt. Combine the molasses, honey and water. Into a bowl add the sifted and liquid ingredients to the butter until well blended. Bake in a greased pan for one hour. Enjoy!

Pioneer Children of Appalachia *(cont.)*

- In the story the children had a wonderful time making corn husk dolls. Allow students to make their very own corn husk dolls by following these directions.

Materials: corn husks (available in grocery stores in Mexican food sections); string or yellow yarn; paints; scissors; paper towels; bucket or pan to soak corn husk; cloth or sponge; cotton, fabric or yarn

1. Prepare the husks by soaking them in water until they are soft (up to one hour). Drain husks on paper towels. Keep the husks damp while working with them.

2. Put six corn husks together and tie a string around the middle for the doll's waist. Tie another piece of string about 2" (5 cm) below the first to form the body. Fold the ends of the husk down from the top and hold them down by tying them in place with another string placed on top of the first string that was tied in the middle.

3. To form the arms and hands, put two husks together and tie them near the ends with strings. Roll and slip the arms through the opening in the top of the body near the neck. To form legs and feet, divide the husks and tie them near the bottom with string.

4. Now paint a face and, if available, use fabric to dress.

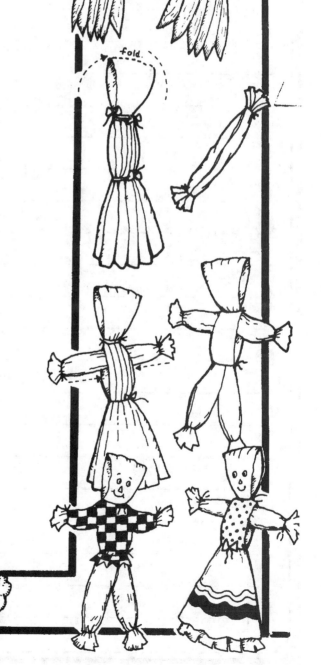

Stories from Our Past

In the space provided, write the story you were told by your grandparent or another adult.

Pioneers

Author: Dennis B. Fradin

Publisher: Childrens Press, Chicago, 1984. 45 pages

Summary: The book provides basic information about the pioneers and their motivation to explore new lands. Ancient pioneers as well as pioneers in America are discussed.

Learning Activities:

- Have students list reasons why people have the desire to move to new places in both the past and the present. They can use a contrast chart like the example below.

Reasons why people moved in the past	Reasons why people move in the present day
People moved to find new farm land.	People moved to find new jobs.

- Using the covered wagon form on page 62 have students list different pioneers and what they discovered. They can use examples from the book as well as doing some research on their own. Several famous pioneers mentioned in the book include: Eric the Red, Leif Ericsson, Daniel Boone, Davy Crockett, and Marcus Whitman. Together the wagons will make an attractive bulletin board display.

- Have students in small groups discuss at what point a pioneer becomes an "invader."

- Early settlers had the opportunity to decide on town names. If students were able to name three local towns, ask them what they would name the towns and why.

- Challenge students to make rafts using small sticks, twigs, and string. Then have a contest to see which rafts float and which rafts sink.

- Have students play the pioneer trivia game on pages 63 and 64. Each group of students can create their own game, ranging from a board game to a flash card game to a game in which points for correct answers are accumulated to determine a winner. The trivia cards can be cut out and laminated for added durability. Answers can be reproduced and glued onto the back of the cards. Students can create additional cards to challenge one another. The answers to the questions are:
1. pioneer 2. Jamestown 3. explorers 4. wagon train 5. Daniel Boone 6. disease
7. Africa, Asia, and Europe 8. Oklahoma 9. Hawaii 10. Spaniards.

Covered Wagons

Using the covered wagon below, write the name of a famous pioneer and draw or describe what that person discovered or accomplished.

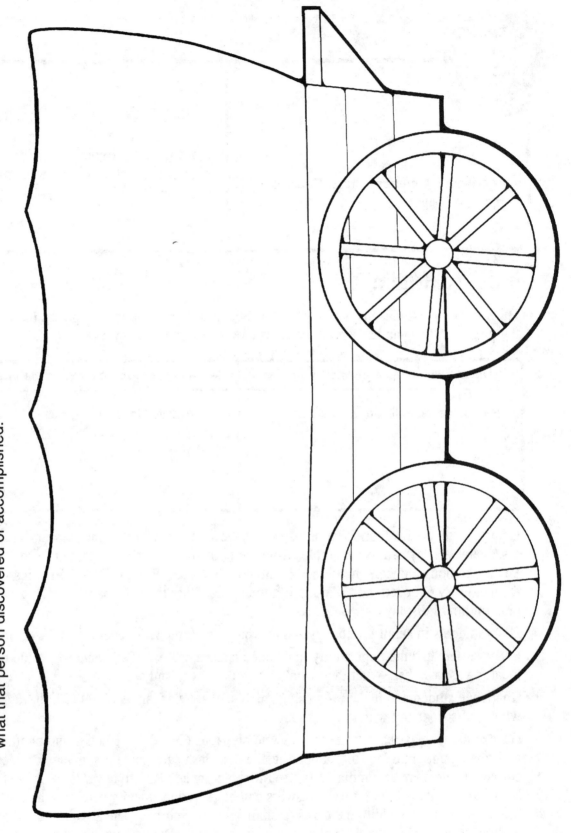

62

Pioneer Trivia Questions

1. What word comes from the Latin word "foot" and describes a person who is one of the first to do something?

2. What was the first permanent English settlement in America?

3. What word describes people who investigate new areas?

4. What were long lines of covered wagons called?

5. Who was the pioneer who always felt crowded?

6. What was the leading cause of death for people on the Oregon Trail?

7. The first people on Earth probably lived on which three continents?

8. What was one of the last places on the mainland of America to be settled by pioneers?

9. What area was named after Hawaiki?

10. What group of people established the first permanent European settlement in America?

Pioneer Trivia Answers

pioneer	explorers
Daniel Boone	Africa, Asia, and Europe
Hawaii	Jamestown
wagon trains	disease
Oklahoma	Spaniards

Save Queen of Sheba

Author: Louise Moeri

Publisher: Dutton, New York, 1981.
92 pages

Summary: Two young children, King David and Queen of Sheba, are the only survivors after the Sioux Indians attack their wagon train. Now, they must move west to Oregon on their own. This is an exciting adventure story children will undoubtedly enjoy.

Learning Activities:

- King David and Queen of Sheba are certainly unique names. Challenge students to ask their parents about the history of their own name, or to research its origin on their own.

- In small groups have students discuss whether or not it was appropriate for King David to hit Queen of Sheba with a stick when she refused to obey him.

- Have students create a special holiday to honor those who lost their lives when the Sioux attacked.

- After all the children had been through in their quest to reach Oregon, they must have been a real sight to their Pa. Have students draw King David and Queen of Sheba as they would have looked when Pa spotted them.

- Challenge students to research any of the Native Americans mentioned in the novel to find out about customs, traditions, clothing, population, etc. Those mentioned include: Brule Sioux, Piegan, Pawnee, Arapaho, Blackfeet, Crow, and Cheyenne.

- Students know what a struggle it was to travel west to Oregon. Allow them to play the Oregon Trail game on pages 66 and 67. The object of the game is to reach Oregon first. Students roll a die and move the number of spaces indicated. The game works best for two to three players.

- Give students the opportunity to taste cornmeal mush by allowing them to prepare and sample some. An easy recipe for cornmeal mush can be found on page 68.

- King David gets to the point several times during the journey when he wonders whether or not he can continue to put up with Queen of Sheba's antics. Write David a letter offering suggestions for dealing with someone who constantly irritates you.

Quest for

Roll a die and move the number of spaces indicated. The game works best for two to three players.

		Sign of Life. *Move Ahead 1.*	
START →			
FINISH Oregon			
Sheba is Missing. *Move Back 1.*			
	Extra Food. *Move Ahead 1.*		**Lost Trail.** *Move Back 1.*

Oregon

Found a Horse.

Move Ahead 1.

Fever Strikes.

Move Back 1.

Sheba is Missing.

Move Back 1.

Wagon Wheels

Author: Barbara Brenner

Illustrator: Don Bolognese

Publisher: Harper and Row, New York, 1978. 64 pages

Summary: A father and his three sons struggle to move west for free land. This is a suspenseful story of a father who has to leave his children while venturing west until he finds a home for the family.

Learning Activities:

- Have students design a poster advertising free land in the West.
- The weather was often bad as the family made their way West. Have students brainstorm a list of things to do when the weather is too bad to be able to go outside to play.
- Have students discuss whether or not it is appropriate to leave an 11, 8, and 3 year-old home alone to take care of themselves.
- Allow students to make cornmeal mush using the recipe below.

Cornmeal Mush

Ingredients: 4 cups (960 mL) water, 1 teaspoon (5 mL) salt, 1 cup (240 mL) stone ground yellow cornmeal, syrup

Directions: Bring four cups of water to a boil in a three quart (284 L) pot. Stir in salt. While stirring the water sprinkle in cornmeal. When all the meal has been stirred in, reduce heat. Simmer for one hour. Stir every ten minutes. Add syrup to taste. The mush is done when it looks like cooked oatmeal. Makes six servings.

- Students who enjoy performing in front of the class will enjoy the reader's theater script on pages 69-71. Reader's theater is an informal type of dramatic play. Students need not memorize the script and props are not necessary; rather their use is usually pantomimed. Students should use body and facial expressions to convey the meaning and mood. Note: The girls can become boys and sons.

Reader's Theater

Wagon Wheels

Scene One

Dad: There it is, boys. Across the river is Nicodemus, Kansas. That is where we are going to build our house. There is free land for everyone here in the West. All we have to do is go and get it.

Johnny: It sure has been a hard trip, Dad.

Dad: Come on, boys. Let's put our feet on free dirt. All we have to do is cross this river.

Sam: Welcome! I'm Sam Hickman. Welcome to the town of Nicodemus.

Dad: Why, thank you, brother. Where exactly is your town?

Sam: Right here!

Johnny: But I don't see any houses.

Dad: Shucks! Holes in the ground are for rabbits and snakes, not for free black people. I am a carpenter. I can build fine wood houses for this town.

Sam: No time to build houses now. Winter is coming and winter in Kansas is mean. Better get yourself a dugout before the ground freezes.

Willie: Whatever you say, Dad.

Dad: We will have to get busy in order to beat the cold weather. O.K. boys. Let's get the shovels and start digging.

Scene Two

Dad: You boys did a good job with this here house.

Johnny: I'm glad we have the dugout to shield us from the cold even if it has a dirt floor and dirt walls.

Willie: I'm going to light the lamp and make a fire.

Johnny: Great! I'll start making rabbit stew and fish.

Dad: After dinner I'll sing a song or two.

Reader's Theater (cont.)

Wagon Wheels (cont.)

Scene Three

Dad: This winter is even meaner than I thought it would be.

Johnny: We haven't had fish or rabbit stew in ages.

Willie: I'm getting tired of eating cornmeal mush!

Dad: Well, there isn't much left of the mush either. We are about to run out of food.

Brother: I'm cold and hungry.

Dad: Let me wrap some blankets around you. Hush, baby son. Try to sleep. Supply train will be coming soon.

Scene Four

Willie: Dad, wake up. I think I hear something.

Dad: Oh Lord! Indians!

Johnny: I'll get my gun, Daddy.

Dad: Hold on, Johnny. Wait and see what they do.

Willie: They are making a circle. Now they are each dropping something on the ground. Now they're coming for us!!

Dad: Calm down, son. I think they are leaving.

Johnny: They are gone, Dad. Can we see what they left?

Dad: Alright, let's see.

Willie: Look! Fresh deer meat and fish.

Brother: And dried beans and squash.

Johnny: And bundles of sticks to keep our fires burning.

Dad: Boys, I want you to remember this day. When someone says bad things about Indians, tell them the Osage Indians saved our lives in Nicodemus.

Reader's Theater *(cont.)*

Wagon Wheels *(cont.)*

Scene Five

Dad: Boys, this prairie is too flat for me. I want to find land with trees and hills. I'm going to move on.

Johnny: I will start loading the wagon.

Dad: Hold on now. I want you boys to stay. You have shelter and friends here. I will go alone and send for you when I find a place.

Willie: We'll be scared!

Dad: Don't worry. I'll leave you cornmeal, salt, and molasses. You be good boys, you hear?

Boys: Don't leave, Daddy!

Dad: I have to. It's for the good of the family.

Boys: Good-bye, Daddy!

Scene Six

Johnny: Willie, Little Brother, look! It's a letter from dad. He found a place near Solomon City, and he wants us to use this map to find and join him.

Willie: Are you sure you can follow the map?

Johnny: Of course!

Scene Seven

Boys: Daddy!

Dad: Willie! Johnny! Little Brother! You made it!

Johnny: We sure missed you, Daddy.

Dad: I'm glad we're all together again!

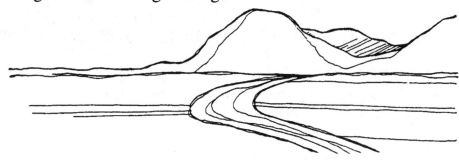

Little House in the Big Woods

Author: Laura Ingalls Wilder

Illustrator: Garth Williams

Publisher: HarperCollins, New York, 1932. 238 pages

Summary: This book is a touching, true story of the childhood of Laura Ingalls Wilder and her family of early pioneers.

Learning Activities:

(Chapters 1-4)

- Have students write a research report on any of the animals mentioned in the story. The list of animals includes: wolves, bears, wild cats, deer, muskrats, mink, otters, foxes, squirrels, rabbits, chipmunks, and panthers. The students should answer the questions on the activity sheet on page 77.

- Laura and her sisters called their parents Ma and Pa. Brainstorm with students different ways in which to say mother and father. Students from other cultures will probably have some wonderful suggestions.

- The Ingalls family could not afford to waste anything. When a pig was killed, everything was used. The bladder became a toy for Laura and Mary and the young girls feasted on the tail. Have students in small groups discuss what we can learn from the Ingalls' about conservation and waste.

- It was a real treat when Pa played his fiddle for the family. They often enjoyed a round of "Yankee Doodle." (The music and words can be found in *Gonna Sing My Head Off* by Kathleen Krull, Knopf, 1992.) As a class, sing this popular tune.

- Pa fascinated the children with stories from his own childhood and his father's childhood. Have students write one of their own favorite childhood stories to be preserved and someday told to their children or grandchildren.

- Ask students to discuss in small groups whether or not they thought it was fair for Laura to receive an "extra" Christmas present. Laura received a special doll.

Little House in the Big Woods (cont.)

- Laura and Mary were delighted when their mother made them a pancake man. Pancake mix is easily obtained and made, so students can make their own pancake men. However, for the full story and the Ingalls' recipe for pancake men, consult *The Little House Cookbook* by Barbara M. Walker (HarperCollins, 1979).

- When Christmas time was approaching, the weather was quite severe. The Ingalls' house was practically buried in the snow. Children can make a "snow house" with just a little help. (Although it is a simple task, this activity can be messy. Parent volunteers should be solicited!) Using the small milk cartons that often come with school lunches, students can make a simple house.

   Materials: small milk cartons, butter cream frosting (this can be canned), graham crackers, spreaders, small candies such as red hots

   1. Using butter cream frosting, stick graham crackers to the sides and top of the milk carton.

   2. Cover the graham crackers with more frosting to look like snow. Small candies such as red hots and dots can be used to decorate the house. These candies will easily stick to the butter cream frosting.

   3. Voila! A miniature version of the Ingalls' home during the winter.

   4. As an extension, students may wish to create a big woods to place these houses in.

- If you have access to snow, students can make snow candy. Have students collect clean snow and then pour hot maple syrup over it. If snow isn't available, use crushed ice. Although the texture will be different, it will give students a somewhat similar experience. This was a special treat for Laura and Mary.

(Chapters 5-8)

- If it weren't for the lantern, Laura and her mother may not have realized that it was a bear, not their cow, outside the barn. Students can make a basic lantern by following these simple directions.

   1. Fold a piece of rectangular construction paper in half lengthwise. Beginning at the folded edge, cut lines approximately one inch (2.54 cm) apart. These lines should be cut to a point about one inch from the end of the paper.

   2. Open up the paper and glue or staple the sides together forming a lantern. For a handle, glue a strip of construction paper to each side of the top of the lantern.

Little House in the Big Woods *(cont.)*

- Now that students have had the opportunity to get to know Laura and Mary in more detail, have them complete the character chart on page 78.

- Have students brainstorm things they could do if they had to follow the "Sunday" rules of the Ingalls' household.

- Pa enjoyed telling stories to his children. Students can take turns reading settler stories to each other from the *Early Settler Storybook* by Bobbie Kalman (Crabtree Publishing, 1982).

- Laura could not wait for the snow to melt so she could play outside. She hoped for sunny days to melt the snow. Have students conduct an experiment to see how quickly the sun can melt ice. Place an ice cube in a plastic tray in the sun. Have students watch to see how long it takes to melt the ice cube. Then perform the same experiment in the classroom to see how long it takes to melt. Finally, see how long it takes the ice cube to melt when placed in a dark closet. Students can graph the results.

- The Ingalls family was excited about the special dance. Using the outlines on page 79, have students design clothes for Ma, Pa, Mary, and Laura to wear to the dance.

- Obtain some square-dance music complete with calls and allow students to have their own special dance.

- Food played a large part in the Ingalls' family life. Try another cooking experience with your class. Allow students to make hasty pudding. The recipe is easy.

Hasty Pudding

Ingredients: 4 cups (960 mL) water, 1 teaspoon (5 mL) salt, 1 cup (240 mL) stone ground yellow cornmeal, maple syrup

Directions: Bring 4 cups (960 mL) of water to a boil in a 3 quart (2.84 L) pot or kettle. Stir in salt. While stirring the water with a spoon, sprinkle in the cornmeal. Then, reduce heat and simmer for at least an hour, stirring every ten minutes. The hasty pudding is done when it looks like cooked oatmeal. Serve with syrup on top. (Makes six small servings.)

- Have students make clove apples as presents. Stick cloves into the skin of the apple for a sweet-smelling, inexpensive gift.

Little House in the Big Woods (cont.)

(Chapters 9-13)

- Laura was amazed when she saw the store and town for the first time. Have students write a diary entry as if they were Laura for that special day.

- Challenge students to make a diorama of the town store including the many treats inside.

- Whenever Laura and Mary received special cookies from Mrs. Peterson, they always agonized over how much to give baby Carrie. They usually each gave her one-half, but they knew that wasn't fair. Challenge students to compute how much of the two cookies each of the three girls should receive to make it fair and equal.

- Laura wonders if the moon is made of green cheese. Offer a small prize to the first student who can discover of what the moon is made.

- When Mary told Laura that golden curls are much prettier than brown curls, Laura slapped her. She was promptly whipped by her father. In small groups, have students determine a less violent punishment for Laura. Also, have them discuss if Mary should be reprimanded as well.

- Cousin Charley was a real troublemaker. He lied several times to his father which caused his father to ignore Charley's screams for help when Charley really was in trouble. He was stung by hundreds of bees! Ask students whether or not Laura's father showed a good example by not feeling sorry for Charley, and instead calling him a "little liar."

- Pa was thrilled to be able to use the modern threshing machine to help him with his crop. Have students brainstorm other modern inventions that would have made farming much easier for Pa and the Ingalls family.

- Encourage students to read other books by Laura Ingalls Wilder including: *Little House on the Prairie, Farmer Boy, On the Banks of Plum Creek, By the Shores of Silver Lake, The Long Winter, Little Town on the Prairie, These Happy Golden Years,* and *The First Four Years.*

- Encourage students to find out about how the stories of Laura Ingalls Wilder came to be published.

- Have students read the biography of *Laura Ingalls Wilder* written by Patricia Reilly Giff (Puffin, 1987).

Little House in the Big Woods *(cont.)*

- When fall came around, there were plenty of leaves on the ground. Laura used leaves to make hats for her doll and wooden men. Students can use leaves to make prints by following the directions below.

Materials: variety of leaves, tempera paints, large foil pan, newspaper, construction paper, rolling pin, waxed paper, soap, water, and paper towels for clean up

1. Cover work surface with newspaper; then pour tempera paint into large foil pan.

2. Carefully lay a leaf on the surface of the paint. Lift the leaf out of the paint and let the excess paint drip off.

3. With the paint-side down, press the leaf on a piece of construction paper. Lay waxed paper over the leaf and move the rolling pin back and forth.

4. When the print is dry, it may be cut out.

- If your students would like to learn more songs that Laura and her family enjoyed, you may wish to obtain *The Laura Ingalls Wilder Songbook* by Eugenia Carson (Harper, 1968).

- If students want to find out more about Laura Ingalls Wilder on their own, they can write to the Almanzo and Laura Ingalls Wilder Association at P.O. Box 283 Malone, New York 12953.

- As an extension activity, encourage students to read *West from Home: Letters of Laura Ingalls Wilder* (Harper, 1974).

- Have students choose their favorite scene from the book and rewrite it as a reader's theater script. Then have them perform these scenes.

Laura's Furry Friends

Research any of the following animals that frequented the land around the Ingalls' house.

> * Wolf   * Bear   * Wildcat
>
> * Deer   * Muskrat   * Mink
>
> * Otter   * Fox   * Squirrel
>
> * Rabbit   * Chipmunk   * Panther

1. Name the animal you chose to research. _____

2. In what areas of the United States can that animal be found? _____

   _____

3. What does the animal eat? _____

   _____

4. What does the animal use for shelter? _____

   _____

5. Who or what are the animal's enemies? _____

   _____

6. What type of climate does the animal like best? _____

   _____

7. List some books about the animal, fiction or nonfiction. _____

   _____

   _____

8. Draw a picture of the animal you researched.

Those Ingalls Girls!

Laura and Mary have very distinct personalities and unique ways of interacting with each other. Using the character charts below, note unique characteristics of Laura and Mary. Then, think about how they interact with each other by answering the questions that follow.

Laura	Mary

1. Choose three words that best describe the ways in which Laura interacts with Mary.

   _____

2. Choose three words that best describe the ways in which Mary interacts with Laura.

   _____

3. Do you think age has anything to do with the ways in which they interact with each other? _____

   _____

4. Which of the girls would you most like to have as a friend and why? _____

   _____

   _____

Delightful Dance Designs

Imagine that you are able to design the clothes that the Ingalls' family will wear to the special dance. Using the outlines below, finish designing an outfit for Ma, Pa, Mary, and Laura.

Trouble for Lucy

Author: Carla Stevens

Illustrator: Ronald Himler

Publisher: Houghton Mifflin, Boston, 1979. 80 pages

Summary: This is the story of Lucy, her family, and their travels to Oregon in May, 1843. Lucy's companion, a puppy named Finn, causes all kinds of trouble for Lucy and her family during their journey, but providing endless entertainment for the reader.

Learning Activities:

(Chapters 1-4)

- Lucy is jealous that Prudence has four brothers to play with and to do all the chores. Have students compare the benefits of being an only child with the benefits of coming from a large family.

- Have students write a script for what they think may have taken place between Lucy's Pa and her Uncle John. It is apparent that they had a falling out, but we don't know why. This will be up to the students' imagination to create.

- Ask students if they think Miles should have promised not to tell where Lucy was going, even though she was going to be in real danger.

- Have students put themselves in Lucy's shoes. Then have them discuss in small groups whether or not they would have left the group to find their pet if it were missing.

(Chapters 5-7)

- Have students write a thank-you letter from Lucy to the Indians who saved her.

- Have students discuss whether or not they think two very different people can become very good friends as in the case of Lucy and Prudence.

- Lucy is very excited about the new baby. Have students make a welcome sign from Lucy to the baby.

- Using the activity sheet on page 81, have students predict what will happen in the future to the main characters in the book.

Fortune Telling!

This is your chance to become a fortune teller by predicting what will happen in the future to several main characters from the story. List your predictions; then compare them to the predictions of other classmates.

Predictions for:

_____

Lucy:

_____

Finn:

_____

Miles:

_____

Prudence:

_____

Ma and Pa:

_____

Lucy's Baby Sister:

_____

Bibliography

Alderman, C. L. *Annie Oakley and the World of Her Time.* (Macmillan, 1979)

Alter, Judith. *Women of the Old West.* (Watts, 1989)

Bloch, Louis. *Overland to California in 1859: A Guide for Wagon Train Travelers.* (Bloch, 1983)

Brandt, Keith. *Daniel Boone: Frontier Adventures.* (Troll, 1983)

Brink, Carol Ryrie. *Caddie Woodlawn.* (Macmillan, 1973)

Coerr, Eleanora. *The Josephina Quilt Story.* (Harper, 1986)

Cortault, Martine. *Going West: Cowboys and Pioneers.* (Marboro Book, 1989)

Edmonds, Walter. *The Matchlock Gun.* (Putnam, 1941)

Farr, Naunerle C. *Davy Crockett-Daniel Boone.* (Pendulum, 1979)

Fleischman, Sid. *By the Great Horn Spoon!* (Little, Brown, 1963)

Freedman, Russell. *Children of the Wild West.* (Clarion, 1983)

Freedman, Russell. *Cowboys of the Wild West.* (Clarion, 1985)

Giff, Patricia Reilly. *Laura Ingalls Wilder: Growing Up in the Little House.* (Puffin, 1988)

Harvey, B. *My Prairie Christmas.* (Holiday House, 1990)

Holling C. *Tree in the Trail.* (Houghton & Mifflin, 1990)

Jakes, John. *Susanna of the Alamo.* (Harcourt, Brace, Jovanovich, 1990)

Kellogg, Steven. *Paul Bunyan.* (Morrow, 1984)

Kellogg, Steven. *Johnny Appleseed.* (Morrow, 1988)

Lawler, Laurie. *Daniel Boone.* (Whitman, 1989)

Levine, Ellen. *If You Traveled West in a Covered Wagon.* (Scholastic, 1976)

MacLachlan, Patricia. *Sarah, Plain and Tall.* (Harper, 1985)

McNeek, May. *California Gold Rush.* (Random, 1987)

Moseley, Elizabeth. *Davy Crockett: Hero of the Wild Frontier.* (Chelsea, 1991)

O'Dell, Scott. *Streams to the River, River to the Sea.* (Houghton Mifflin, 1986)

Speare, Elizabeth. *Calico Captive.* (Houghton Mifflin, 1957)

Steber, Rick. *Tales of the Wild West* Series, 12 volumes. (Bonanza Publishing, 503-447-3115)

Stewart, George. *The Pioneers Go West.* (Random, 1982)

Taylor, Theodore. *Walking Up a Rainbow.* (Delacorte, 1986)

Turner, A. *Grasshopper Summer.* (Macmillan, 1989)

VanSteenwyk, Elizabeth. *California Gold Rush: West with the Forty-Niners.* (Watts, 1991)

Walker, Barbara M. *The Little House Cookbook.* (Harper, 1979)

Will You Sign Here, John Hancock?

Author: Jean Fritz

Illustrator: Trina Schart Hyman

Publisher: Putnam, New York, 1976. 47 pages

Summary: This book provides a brief history of the life of John Hancock written by historical novelist Jean Fritz.

Learning Activities:

- It would seem as though John Hancock had everything he wanted. He had fine clothes, servants, and a great deal of money. Have students discuss whether or not these material objects made John Hancock happy.

- Have students write a letter to John Hancock from his Uncle Thomas scolding him for his extravagance.

- Have students research why men wore wigs during this time period.

- John Hancock was adamantly opposed to being taxed by the British. Have students consider the ways in which John's feelings about taxes are the same or different from the way people feel about taxes today. You may wish to encourage students to locate articles on new taxes in the newspapers.

- The Tories often wrote nasty things about John Hancock in their newspaper, as well as drawing silly pictures of him. Have students write a newspaper article for either the Tory paper denouncing Hancock or a fictitious paper that supports Hancock. Students should also be encouraged to draw a picture of Hancock. Use page 85 as a template for the article.

- During the height of his frustration with Hancock, the King put a price of 500 pounds on Hancock's head. Using the exchange rates in the newspaper, have students find out how much 500 pounds would be worth in American dollars.

- John Hancock liked to experiment in signing his name in different ways. Have students practice signing their names in different and unique ways.

Will You Sign Here, John Hancock? *(cont.)*

- John Hancock dressed very flamboyantly. On page 86 are outlines for several of his outfits. Have students color in these outfits using descriptions from the book, or a design of their own. These can be cut out and made into a bulletin board.

- Have students consider whether or not they think it was appropriate for John Hancock to give away expensive gifts in hopes of receiving votes.

- Have students hold a mock Congressional meeting to debate whether Americans should seek their independence. Students can take turns playing different roles.

- John Hancock's idea of "roughing it" meant eating without a tablecloth, putting out his own candle, and serving his gravy with a pewter spoon. Ask students to compare their ideas of "roughing it" with John Hancock's. Then, they may write a brief report of the differences.

- When John Hancock became governor, he ordered all new home furnishings along with other extravagant items. Have students develop a petition against John Hancock as members of the community who oppose him for spending so much money.

- John Hancock was so concerned with his popularity that he always tried to please everyone. Ask students to respond in writing to this question: "Why is it a bad idea for a politician to try to please everyone?"

- Plumcake was a popular treat during this time period. A recipe for baked plum pudding (a little easier to prepare than plumcake) can be found below.

Baked Plum Pudding

Ingredients:

- ¹/₂ cup (120 mL) butter
- 6 eggs,
- 1 tablespoon (15 mL) flour
- 2 teaspoons (10 mL) cinnamon
- ¹/₂ teaspoon (2.5 mL) allspice *(Serves ten.)*

- 1 cup (240 mL) sugar
- 1 cup (240 mL) raisins, currants, and pecans
- 2 cups (480 mL) bread crumbs
- ¹/₂ teaspoon (2.5 mL) cloves

Directions: Preheat oven to 375 F degrees (191 C°). Beat butter in bowl until soft. Add sugar gradually and cream. Beat in eggs one at a time. Combine raisins, currants, and pecans and sprinkle lightly with flour in a separate bowl. Add to butter mixture. Combine bread crumbs, cinnamon, cloves, and allspice in a third bowl and add to butter mixture. Bake in a greased pan for 30 minutes.

Makes 10 servings.

- Have students write a eulogy for John Hancock. Those who volunteer can deliver the eulogy in front of the class.

American Revolution

EXTRA! EXTRA!

Write a newspaper article about John Hancock. You can either write for a Tory paper and denounce Hancock, or write for a fictitious paper that supports Hancock. Write it in the newspaper outline below, and include a picture and a caption.

A Fine Wardrobe

Using the outlines below, design several flamboyant outfits for John Hancock to wear. You may wish to use the descriptions of his clothes from the book for ideas.

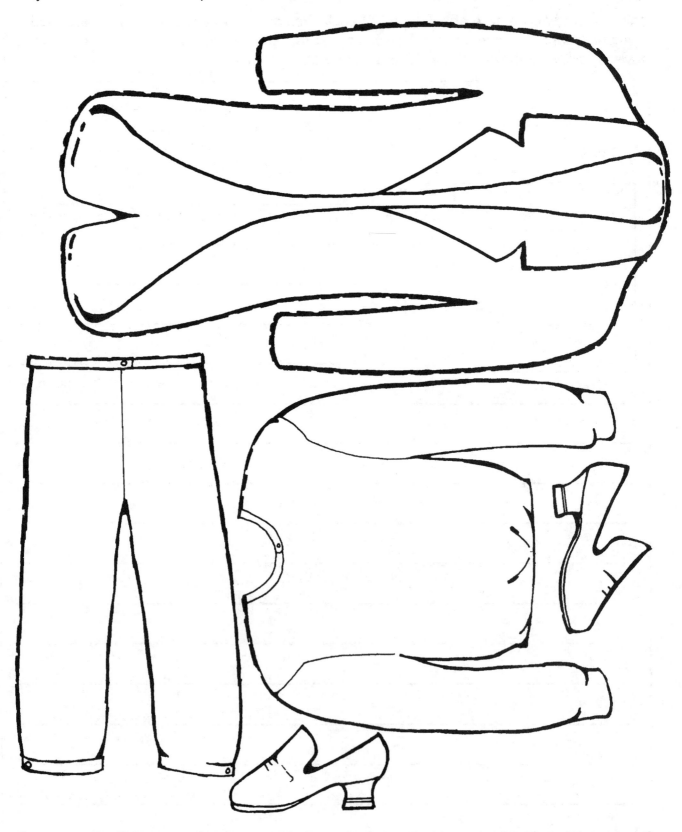

My Brother Sam Is Dead

Author: James Lincoln Collier and Christopher Collier

Publisher: Macmillan, New York, 1974. 211 pages

Summary: Sam has chosen to fight as a Rebel in the Revolutionary War against his family's wishes. However, when Sam is accused by his people of a crime he didn't commit, he wonders whether or not his decision to fight in the war was a wise one.

Learning Activities:

(Chapters 1-5)

- Sam is a debater at college. Have students choose a topic they feel strongly about and debate it with a friend who disagrees. The debate should be carried out before the class, who after listening to both sides, will determine who won. Prior to the debate, the students should determine how they will decide who wins. You may also wish to have students decide what a "telling point" is. This activity will be good practice for another debate activity to take place after completion of the book.

- Have students determine a topic that they do not agree on with their parents. Then have students write a persuasive letter to their parents trying to convince their parents to see their side.

- Using the descriptions given in the first chapter, have students draw the tavern.

- During the time period of the story there was a law forcing people to attend church. Have students research other laws from earlier time periods. (A good reference book on this subject is *Crazy Laws* by Dick Hyman, Scholastic, 1978.) Then, have students write a persuasive speech as if they are a lawyer trying to get an old law repealed.

- Timmy liked to swim in streams, climb trees, and spin tops for recreation. As a class, have students brainstorm types of recreational activities they enjoy. How do they differ from Timmy's activities?

- Sam suggested that he joined the war effort because all his college friends did. Have students write about something they did just because all their friends did. Ask them to consider whether or not it was a good idea to follow their friend's lead in the situation.

My Brother Sam Is Dead *(cont.)*

- Timmy was very excited to read the almanac. Introduce students to the almanac by having them answer the questions below.

    What type of information do you find in an almanac?

    How is the information organized?

    How often is the almanac published?

- Have students compose questions that could be answered by using an almanac.

- Timmy always wants to compete with Sam. Have students think about this situation. Let them give advice to Sam by writing a short answer response.

- Use the following discussion questions for chapters 1-5.

    Is it worth dying to be free?

    Do you think children should keep their opinions to themselves in front of adults?

    If you were Timmy, what side would you choose and why?

    Is Sam a man because he joined the army?

(Chapters 6-10)

- Messengers were constantly sending secret messages back and forth on both sides. Have students design a secret code. Then have them write a secret message using the code. Their partner will receive the message and the code, and will then have to determine the secret message.

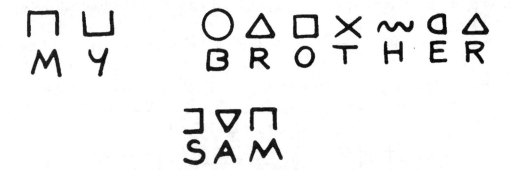

- The cowboys often took supplies from unsuspecting travelers. Have students imagine that they are a judge and write a decision regarding the punishment of any cowboys caught stealing from travelers.

- Timmy thought it was fun to visit his relatives because he was able to catch up on all the family news. Have students create a family newsletter for their own families using the template on page 90.

- Using Timmy's vivid descriptions, have students draw the Hudson river or create a diorama of it.

- Eating Johnny cakes was popular during the time of the Revolutionary War. Have students prepare Johnny cakes by following the recipe in *The Little House Cookbook* by Barbara M. Walker (HarperCollins, 1979).

My Brother Sam Is Dead (cont.)

- Timmy amused himself during his long journey by trying to name all the countries. Have students brainstorm on their own and try to name as many countries as they can. Then, as a group, see how many countries the entire class can list. Reproduce twice and cut out the cards on pages 91-92. Have students shuffle the cards and lay all cards face down on a table. Then have them take turns turning over two cards at a time. After they see the name of the country, they should turn the cards over. Students must try to remember where the country cards are located. The object of the game is to get a match of two country cards.

(Chapters 11-14)

- Have students write Sam a letter from his mother trying to convince him to come home because their father is now in prison and the family needs help.

- Have students stage a memorial ceremony for all those who lost their lives in the Revolutionary War.

- Sam is in desperate trouble since being imprisoned for stealing the family cows. Have students prepare a defense for Sam's court martial. They should give the speech before a panel of students who will then be charged with deciding Sam's fate.

- Have students write a descriptive poem describing what either Sam, Timmy, or their mother is feeling the night before Sam is scheduled to be killed.

- Have students write an essay explaining whether they would be a Tory or a Rebel. Then have students debate with each other. A panel should be chosen to decide which person wins each debate and to keep track of all the "telling points."

- Have students write a eulogy for Sam from Timmy's point of view.

- Have students discuss the following questions in small groups or as a whole class:

    Do you think it is fair to "make an example" of someone?

    Given the nonsupport of his own party, do you think Sam regretted joining the Rebels?

    What do you think Timmy's father meant when he said, "In war the dead pay the debts of the living"?

Family Newsletter

Using the following template, write a newsletter that can be distributed to all your family members.

The _____ Family

Newsletter

Country Concentration

See directions on page 89.

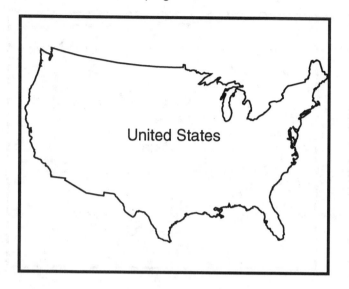

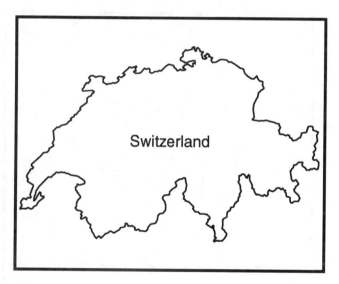

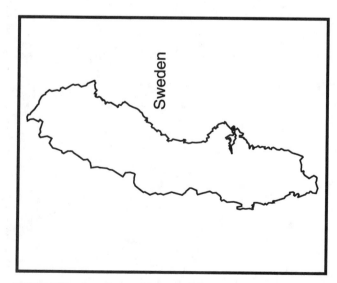

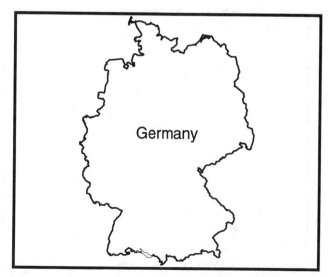

Country Concentration *(cont.)*

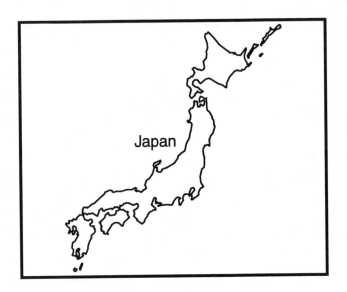

Japan

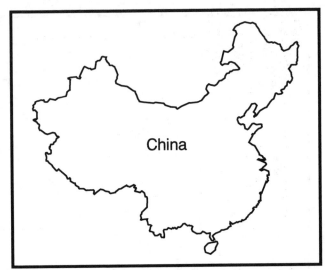

China

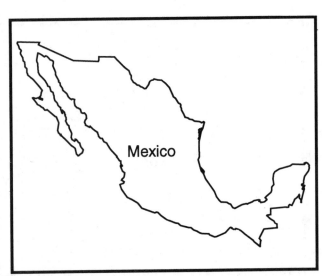

Mexico

Argentina

Spain

Can't You Make Them Behave, King George?

Author: Jean Fritz

Illustrator: Tomie DePaola

Publisher: Scholastic, New York, 1977. 46 pages

Summary: This book provides an accounting of the events leading up to the American Revolution as told by the popular historical novelist Jean Fritz. Illustrations by Tomie DePaola enliven the story.

Learning Activities:

- Have students write a news article comparing the styles of King George II and King George III. Suggest that they use some of John Hancock's quotes from the book.

- Have students draw a fancy wedding portrait of King George II and his bride, Princess Charlotte.

- Challenge students to locate the words to "God Save the King."

- Have students in small groups discuss whether or not they think it was fair for Americans to be taxed. Remind them that the tax was supposed to pay for the war and to protect the Americans.

- When King George wanted to forget about being a king he would play backgammon. Challenge students to learn to play backgammon. Then this game can be played during classroom free time.

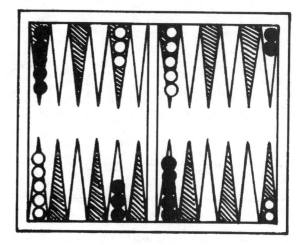

- Have students brainstorm the ways in which the jobs of the king and the president are similar.

- King George wrote a letter to the Secretary of state of America encouraging him to continue with the war. Have students write this letter as the King would have written it.

- In small groups, have students discuss conflict resolution. Encourage them to use the information on the activity sheet located on page 94.

Solving a Dispute

King George had difficulty getting the Americans to pay the taxes that he felt they owed. In order to force the Americans into paying the taxes a war began. The result was that the colonies severed all ties with England and the King. Consider other ways the King may have gone about resolving the conflict. Read the suggestions below; then answer the questions that follow.

Conflict Resolution Strategies

Compromise: Both parties give up something and both get something in return.

Postpone: Put off resolving the conflict until both parties are more in control.

Share: Make people's feelings the top priority.

Chance: Flip a coin.

Get Help: Seek advice from a neutral party.

Avoid: Avoid the conflict all together.

Apologize: Say I'm sorry.

---

1. Which strategies could the King have used to resolve the conflict? _____

   _____

   _____

2. Which single strategy do you think would have worked best for the King? _____

   _____

   _____

3. Which conflict resolution strategies have you used in the past? _____

   _____

   _____

4. Which strategy do you think is the best way to resolve most conflicts? _____

   _____

   _____

5. In the next few days, observe potential conflicts on the playground. Note what the conflict was about and how the parties went about trying to resolve it.

The Story of the Declaration of Independence

Author: Norman Richards

Illustrator: Tom Dunnington

Publisher: Childrens Press, Chicago, 1968. 31 pages

Summary: The story provides a look at why and how the Declaration of Independence came into existence beginning with the Pilgrims landing at Plymouth in 1620. A copy of the Declaration of Independence appears at the beginning of the book.

Learning Activities:

- On the first page of the book, the Mayflower Compact is discussed. It mentions that the Compact guaranteed that each man had the right to vote. Discuss with students what this really meant. Challenge them to find out when blacks and women were granted the right to vote.

- Have students make a map of the thirteen colonies.

- A common chore for children was to work in the vegetable garden. Have students plant small vegetable gardens either in the classroom in small plant trays, on the school grounds, or at home.

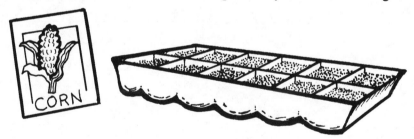

- The soldiers that the King sent were given a paper called Writs of Assistance which allowed them to force themselves into homes. Have students write what they believe these forms may have said.

- The Continental Congress made a list of complaints to send to the King. Have students brainstorm a list of what those complaints may have been.

- Have students meet in small groups to discuss what the classroom rules of behavior should be. The focus should be on negotiation, as it was for the members of the Continental Congress. They may use the form on page 96 to write the rules. When the rules are complete and have been adopted by the class, all should sign the document just like the Declaration of Independence.

- Have students do a research project on any of the Patriot leaders mentioned in the story. Those mentioned include: John Hancock, Samuel Adams, John Adams, Patrick Henry, and Richard Henry Lee.

Declaration of Classroom Rules

Using the form below, draft a list of classroom rules within your small group. You must agree on all the rules within your group before they can be placed on the list. When your list is complete, all members of the group should sign it just like the Declaration of Independence.

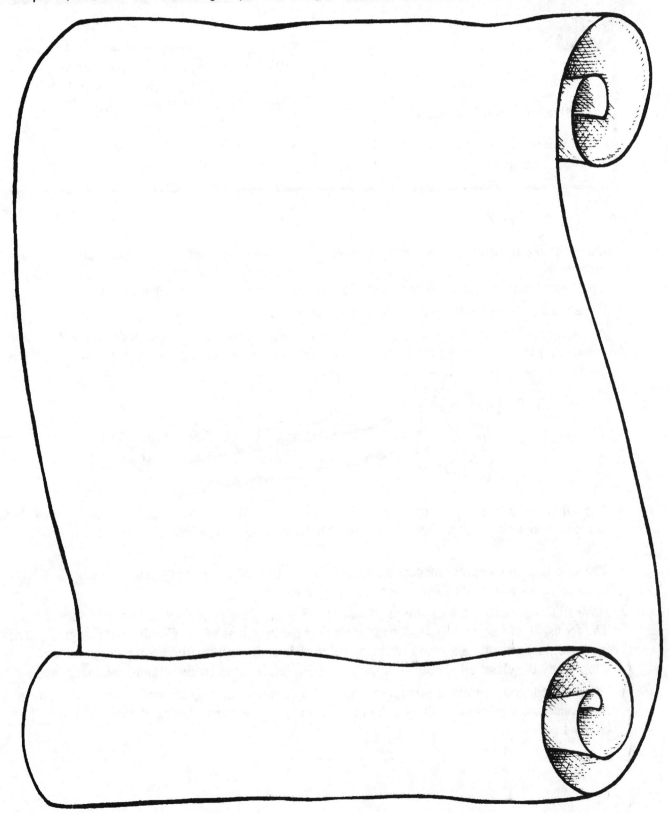

America's Paul Revere

Author: Esther Forbes

Illustrator: Lynd Ward

Publisher: Houghton Mifflin, Boston, 1974. 46 pages

Summary: Inspired by the Pulitzer Prize winning biography, *Paul Revere and the World He Lived In*, this book was written for children and tells the story of Paul Revere's life from age 13 until his death.

Learning Activities:

- At age thirteen Paul Revere did a very brave thing; he took a ship alone to America. Have students write a story about something they did that required bravery.

- Money was very tight when Paul was growing up, so he lived on a tight budget. Have students make their own budget using the activity sheet on page 99.

- Have students brainstorm what qualities make a good soldier.

- When Paul was in school it was common to make students wear dunce caps. There was also corporal punishment during that time. Have students write a letter to the principal of Paul's school declaring their feelings about the dunce caps and severe punishment. Tell them to use their persuasive skills in the letter.

- Paul liked to play marbles and ball games. During the next physical education period, allow students to play a game of marbles or a ball game of their choice.

- Many generations of Paul's family are discussed in the story. Have students make a family tree for Paul Revere.

- When Paul Revere was young he learned how to be a silversmith. However, as silver became more expensive people didn't use it very much; except for teeth. It used to be that people would have bad teeth pulled. However, a technique was developed to fill the bad teeth with silver. So, Paul learned how to be a dentist. Have students design an ad for Paul's dentistry business.

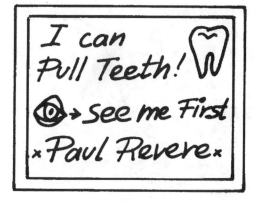

America's Paul Revere *(cont.)*

- John Singleton Copley owed Paul Revere a great deal of money for all the gold frames he purchased from Paul. So, John offered to paint Paul's picture to cancel the debt. Have students draw a picture of Paul and enclose it with a gold frame. They can either use gold construction paper or gold spray paint on white construction paper for the frame.

- In the book it says that Copley painted what Revere looked like as well as his character and principles. Have students meet in small groups to discuss what they think Revere's principles are, based on what they've read in the book.

- Several British soldiers were accused of shooting several young children. There was a dispute, however, as to whether or not they shot in self-defense. Have students hold a mock trial to determine the soldiers' guilt or innocence. The possible roles can be: judge, jury, three soldiers, witnesses, and two attorneys.

- The book describes what the British soldiers looked like, especially when they came in droves. Using the outline on page 100 have students draw the soldiers as described in the story. Then as a class, have students create a mural backdrop. The illustrations from the book can be used as suggestions for the backdrop. Then each student can place the soldier they colored on the mural.

- On the last two pages of *America's Paul Revere* are poems that Paul Revere liked. Have students memorize and recite one of these poems to the class.

- Read to students Henry Wadsworth Longfellow's classic *Paul Revere's Ride*.

- Have students design a flag for the newly-free thirteen colonies.

- People died very young during Paul Revere's time. Challenge students to research common diseases that were life threatening during Paul Revere's era.

- Paul Revere was in the silver business. Have students make trinket jewelry out of macaroni and spray paint it silver to look like something that may have come from Paul Revere's shop.

Dollars and Sense

Making and sticking to a budget is serious business. It meant life or death for Paul's family because there was such a shortage of money at that time.

Calculate your monthly allowance. Then list all your expenses, or items you frequently spend your money on. Is there any money left over at the end of the month? Imagine that you have to save a portion of your allowance. With your current budget, are you able to save any money?

Monthly Allowance: _____

Amount you will save each month: _____

Amount left over to spend: _____

Expenses

Item: **Amount:**

_____   _____

_____   _____

_____   _____

_____   _____

_____   _____

_____   _____

_____   _____

                    Total Amount: _____

Soldiers in Droves

Color in the British soldiers outlined below; then cut them out. As a class, make a mural depicting the backdrop of a battleground. Add your soldiers to the mural.

American Revolution Bibliography

Avi. *The Fighting Ground.* (Lippincott, 1984)

Baker, Charles. *The Struggle for Freedom: Plays on the American Revolution.* (Cobblestone, 1990)

Bliven, Bruce Jr. *American Revolution.* (Random, 1963)

Brady, Esther Wood. *Toliver's Secret.* (Crown, 1988)

Brown, Drollen. *Sybil Rides for Independence.* (A. Whitman, 1985)

Clapp, Patricia. *I'm Deborah Sampson: A Soldier in the War of the Revolution.* (Lothrop, 1977)

Clark, Phillip. *American Revolution.* (Marshall Cavendish, 1988)

Collier, James, and Christopher Collier. *Jump Ship to Freedom.* (Delacorte, 1981)

Davis, Burke. *Black Heroes of the American Revolution.* (Harcourt, 1976)

Evans, Elizabeth. *Weathering the Storm: Women of the Revolution.* (Scribner, 1975)

Forbes, Esther. *Johnny Tremain.* (Houghton Mifflin, 1943)

Fritz, Jean. *And Then What Happened Paul Revere?* (Coward, 1973)

Fritz, Jean. *Shh! We're Writing the Constitution.* (Putnam, 1987)

Fritz, Jean. *What's the Big Idea Ben Franklin?* (Coward, 1976)

Knight, James. *Boston Tea Party: Rebellion in the Colonies.* (Troll, 1982)

Lawson, Robert. *Mr. Revere and I.* (Little, Brown, 1953)

Levy, Elizabeth. *If You Were There When They Signed the Constitution.* (Scholastic, 1987)

Longfellow, Henry Wadsworth. *Paul Revere's Ride.* (Dutton, 1990)

Marrin, A. *The War for Independence: The Story of the American Revolution.* (Atheneum, 1988)

McGovern, Ann. *Secret Soldier: The Story of Deborah Sampson.* (Scholastic, 1990)

Meltzer, M. *The American Revolutionaries: A History in Their Own Words.* (Crowell, 1987)

Miller, Natalie. *Story of the Liberty Bell.* (Childrens Press, 1965)

Patterson, Charles. *Thomas Jefferson.* (Watts, 1987)

Reische, Diana. *Patrick Henry.* (Watts, 1987)

Richards, Norman. *Story of the Declaration of Independence.* (Children's Press, 1968)

Sabin, Francene. *American Revolution.* (Troll, 1985)

Stein, Conrad. *Story of Lexington & Concord.* (Children's Press, 1983)

Stone, Melissa. *Rebellion's Song.* (Steck-Vaughn, 1989)

The Perilous Road

Author: William O. Steele

Publisher: Harcourt, Brace & Jovanovich, Orlando, 1958. 156 pages

Summary: Young Chris Brabson finds himself torn over which side is right in the Civil War, and his decision could mean life or death for his brother.

Learning Activities:

(Chapters 1–7)

- The Yankees took items of great value to Chris' family. Have students write about how they would feel if something of personal value was stolen. What if they knew who did it and were not allowed to do anything about it?

- Have students write the conversation that took place between Jethro and his wife and parents when he told them he was joining the Union army.

- Chris felt alone in his contempt for the Yankees. In small groups, have students discuss a time when they felt alone regarding their opinion about something.

- Have students brainstorm what Chris' father could have done when the Yankees robbed him.

- Chris wanted to free the mules the Yankees held to prove his loyalty. Have students devise a plan for Chris to steal the mules.

- Have students discuss the following questions dealing with the events in the first seven chapters:

    Why would Jethro want to join the Yankees?

    Was it appropriate for the Brabson's neighbors to turn against them because of Jethro?

    How should Chris have responded to his friends calling him a blue-belly?

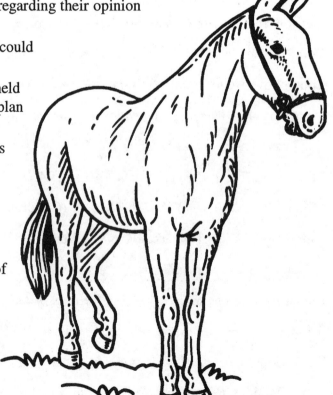

The Perilous Road (cont.)

(Chapters 8-14)

- Chris and his family ate hominy. Have students make hominy using the recipe from *The Little House Cookbook* by Barbara M. Walker (HarperCollins, 1979).

- Leah and Chris enjoyed hearing ghost stories their mother told. Allow students to tell ghost stories to each other with the lights out. A good source book is *Short and Shivery* by Robert D. San Souci (Doubleday, 1987).

- Have students design a "wanted" poster for Yankee soldiers.

- Have students debate whether or not they think Chris should become a spy for Silas.

- Chris was furious about the burning of his family's barn. Have students imagine that Chris was able to confront the people who burned the barn. What would he say to them? How would he handle the situation?

- The Yankee soldiers offered Chris some gingersnaps. Have students make gingersnaps by following this recipe.

Gingersnaps

Ingredients: $^{3}/_{4}$ cup (177 mL) butter, 2 cups (480 mL) sugar, 2 eggs, $^{1}/_{2}$ cup (120 mL) molasses, 2 teaspoons (10 mL) vinegar, 3 $^{3}/_{4}$ cups (480 mL) all purpose flour, 1 $^{1}/_{2}$ teaspoons (8 mL) baking soda, 3 teaspoons (15 mL) ginger, $^{1}/_{2}$ teaspoon (2.5 mL) cinnamon, $^{1}/_{4}$ teaspoon (1.2 mL) cloves

Directions: Preheat oven to 325^{0} F (163^{0} C^{0}). Cream butter and sugar. Stir in eggs (well beaten), molasses, and vinegar. Sift and add remaining ingredients. Mix until well blended. Form dough into balls and cook on greased cookie sheet for 12 minutes.

Makes about 10 dozen.

- Have students write a final chapter to the story in which Jethro's fate is revealed.

- Use the following questions for small group discussion:

    Why were the Yankee soldiers nice to Chris?

    Why would Silas lie about being a spy?

    Will Chris' parents forgive him if Jethro does not return home safely?

The Battle of Gettysburg

Author: Neil Johnson

Publisher: Four Winds Press, New York, 1989. 53 pages.

Summary: In July, 1863, the great battle of Gettysburg was fought. On the battle's anniversary 125 years later, people gathered near the fields where the battle was fought for a reenactment. Photos taken during the reenactment were used to illustrate the story of the battle of Gettysburg in this amazing book.

Learning Activities:

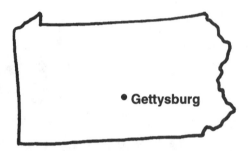

- Locate Gettysburg on a map for students.

- Have students discuss how the North and South became so violently opposed to each other.

- As a presidential candidate, Abraham Lincoln came out against slavery. Have students write a campaign speech for Lincoln to give to the citizens of both the North and the South.

- To accompany Lincoln's speech, have students create a campaign poster for Abraham Lincoln.

- At one point in the battle, General Meade gathered his top generals at his farmhouse quarters to ask for advice. Have students reenact this scene and offer advice to Meade on how to win the battle of Gettysburg.

- When the Confederate soldiers knew the end was near, they began writing last letters to loved ones. Have students write a last letter to a loved one from the point of view of a Confederate soldier.

- On page 55 of *The Battle of Gettysburg* is Lincoln's Gettysburg Address. Students with a flare for the dramatic might enjoy giving this impassioned speech to the class.

- On page 106 is a Gettysburg crossword puzzle based.

  The answers are:

  Across: 1. Stonewall 2. Gettysburg 7. North 10. Confederate 11. South

  Down: 1. South Carolina 3. Robert E. Lee 4. Chamberlain 5. Devil's Den 6. Lincoln 8. Pickett 9. Meade.

Battle of Gettysburg Crossword Puzzle

Based on the facts of the battle of Gettysburg you learned from the book, complete the crossword puzzle below.

Across

1. Nickname of Thomas J. Jackson
2. Civil War's bloodiest battle
7. Region against slavery
10. Army that retreated
11. Region for slavery

Down

1. First state to withdraw from the Union
3. Gray-headed Commander of Confederate troops
4. Maine Commander Colonel Joshua _____
5. Area of giant boulders, jumbled masses of rock and crevices
6. Presidential candidate against slavery
8. Constantly wrote love letters to fiancée
9. Became Commanding General of Union army in June 1863

The Boys' War

Author: Jim Murphy

Publisher: Houghton Mifflin, Boston, 1990. 95 pages

Summary: Riveting stories of the Civil War from soldiers on both the Confederate and Union sides of the battle.

Learning Activities:

(Chapters 1-5)

- Obtain all the words to "Yankee Doodle" and sing it with the class. (The music and words can be found in *Gonna Sing My Head Off* by Kathleen Krull, Knopf, 1992.) After receiving word of Fort Sumter's fall, President Lincoln issued a "call to arms." He needed people to serve in the army. The call was spread by telegraph, newspaper headlines, and bulletins. Have students create any one of these announcements for recruits.

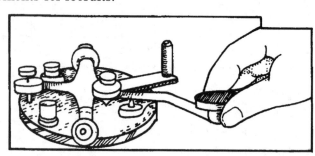

- Have students make contrast charts highlighting the disagreements between the North and the South that led to the war.

- As the recruits started pouring in, they were asked to complete recruitment forms. Have students create a recruitment form for both the Confederate and Union army requesting all the information they deem necessary.

- At first neither side had uniforms. This made it very difficult to tell which side each soldier was on. Have students create a uniform for either or both sides.

- Union soldiers were constantly drilled on procedures and marching. The Confederate soldiers were not. Have students debate in small groups whether or not they think drilling the soldiers was a good idea.

- Many of the soldiers were very homesick. Ask students to imagine what it would be like to be so young and away from home for so long. Then have them write a letter home describing the war and the homesickness as if they were a soldier.

The Boys' War (cont.)

- Many soldiers were left where they were killed. There was no time to bury soldiers. Ask students to write a special poem that soldiers could recite when another passed on.

- Have students design a medal of honor and special certificate for brave soldiers. They may use the template located on page 108.

- As each side needed more officers, soldiers were promoted through the ranks in spite of a lack of leadership skills. Have students work in small groups to determine a guideline of minimum standards for officers in the army.

- Foraging for food was illegal but sometimes quite necessary. Have students draft a law against foraging. Ask them to consider if foraging is always a crime or if there can be special circumstances.

(Chapters 6-10)

- When the soldiers were bored they often played cards and checkers. Allow students to play these games in class after completing their work.

- The soldiers had seen so much death that the sight of a dead body no longer affected them. As a class, discuss how violence in local cities, states, or on television affects our own tolerance levels.

- Henry Wirz was tried for war crimes, namely the horrible prison conditions he forced soldiers to live in. Ask students to decide in small groups what they think his punishment should be.

- Have students research some of the other large battles of the Civil War such as: Shiloh, Antietam, Vicksburg, and Chancellorsville.

- Have students locate the words and then sing "When Johnny Comes Marching Home Again."

- Homecoming receptions for Confederate and Union soldiers were probably very different. Have students choose a side and then write an essay about the reception as if they were there as an observer.

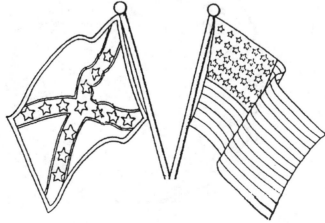

A Badge of Honor

Using the templates below, design a medal of bravery and a special certificate to give to soldiers on either side that are well deserving.

This medal is presented to

_____

for

_____

on

_____

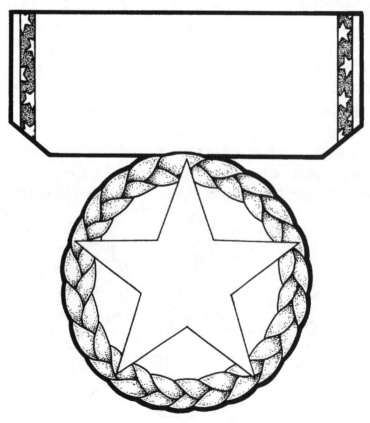

Lincoln: A Photobiography

Author: Russell Freedman

Publisher: Houghton Mifflin, Boston, 1987. 132 pages

Summary: This Newbery Award-winning story of Abraham Lincoln's amazing life is accompanied by prints and photographs.

Learning Activities:

(Chapters 1-3)

- Have students make Lincoln's top hat using the instructions below.

  Materials: black construction paper, tape, scissors

  1. Using a sheet of black construction paper, make a tube large enough to fit around the student's head. Tape or staple together.

  2. Stand the tube on another sheet of black construction paper and trace around the tube. This will become the top of the hat. Tape in place.

  3. Again trace the tube on construction paper with a 1 ½ inch (4 cm) border all the way around to form the hat brim. On this same piece of paper, trace exactly around the tube. Now, have students cut out the center portion so the brim fits around the hat.

  4. Fasten the brim to the hat!

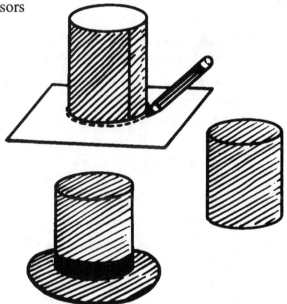

- Because cameras were very primitive during Lincoln's time, there are few good photos of him. Have students draw Lincoln using a pencil and shading.

- Lincoln was described as being extremely superstitious. Have students in small groups discuss the superstitions they know of or believe in.

- Lincoln eventually went on a moral crusade against slavery making speeches all over in front of large crowds. Have students write a speech against slavery. Those with a flare for the dramatic can give this impassioned speech in front of the class.

Lincoln: A Photobiography *(cont.)*

Lincoln lived in a log cabin as a child. Have students make a log cabin using the directions below.

Materials: brown construction paper, glue, white construction paper, crayons, scissors

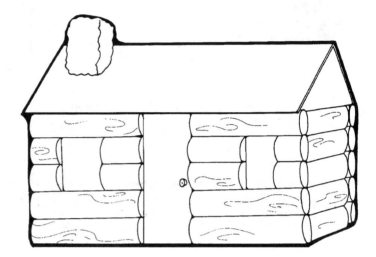

1. Cut out 5" x 9" inch (13 cm x 23 cm) rectangles from brown construction paper. Roll each rectangle into a log and glue in place.

2. Create the front of the cabin by gluing the rolls onto a portion of a 12" x 18" (30 cm x 46 cm) piece of construction paper.

3. Cut out windows, a door, and chimney from scrap pieces of construction paper and glue onto the log cabin.

4. Draw in a background scene onto the piece of construction paper.

- Have students discuss how Lincoln became qualified to be a United States President after having only one year of formal schooling.

- For extra credit, have students read either one of these favorites of Lincoln: *Robinson Crusoe* or *Tales of the Arabian Nights.*

- Lincoln worked very hard to earn money. However, as long as he was living at home, he had to follow the law that required he give all his earnings to his parents. Ask students what they think of this law. How would they feel if they had to give all the money they earned to their parents until they moved out? Why do they think such a law existed?

- When Lincoln was 22 years old, he decided to move out of his parents' house. Have students write a letter from Lincoln to his parents thanking them for all their support for 22 years.

- When Lincoln was 23 years old, he decided to run for the Illinois State Legislature. Have students write a campaign speech for Lincoln.

- When Lincoln lost the election for the State Legislature he had to find work. He did odd jobs such as surveying. Have students design an ad for Lincoln to get work using the activity sheet on page 113.

- The store Lincoln ran with his friend did not do very well. Lincoln was left with a $1,100 debt. At the time, Lincoln was only earning $50 per year. At that rate, have students compute how long it would take Lincoln to pay off his debt.

Lincoln: A Photobiography *(cont.)*

(Chapters 3-4)

- Given the explanation of beliefs for the Democrats and Whigs, ask students which one they would be.

- Lincoln wanted to marry Mary Owens. Unfortunately, her father did not think Lincoln was worthy of her. Have students write the conversation that may have occurred between Mary and her father as they discuss Lincoln and her relationship with him.

- Have students write a letter to Mary's father from Lincoln asking for her hand in marriage.

- Lincoln was opposed to the Mexican War in which the United States tried to gain control of the present areas of California, Utah, Nevada, Arizona, New Mexico and parts of Wyoming and Colorado. Have students do research to find out more about the Mexican War.

- Have students create a newspaper ad for Lincoln and Herndon's law office.

- Have students write the bill that Lincoln introduced to outlaw slavery.

- Slavery was a very impassioned issue. Violence was common when the issue was discussed. Following a speech against slavery, a Senator from Massachusetts was beaten with a cane by a Congressman. Have students meet in small groups to decide what punishment they would give to the Congressman if they were a judge.

- Lincoln and Douglas both campaigned for a Senate seat. Have students make a campaign poster for either one of the candidates. Have a classroom debate in which students can either be Lincoln arguing for freedom or Douglas arguing for popular sovereignty.

- The country was deeply divided about the slavery issue. Using the activity sheet on page 114, have students brainstorm the arguments for and against slavery.

- Lincoln played handball, still a popular game today. Encourage students to play handball during recess or physical education class.

Lincoln: A Photobiography *(cont.)*

(Chapters 5-7)

- Have students work in partner groups. One student will write Lincoln's inaugural address as he or she thinks it may have been written. The partner will be the one to give the speech before the class.

- Lincoln was a novice where war was concerned. Ask students what Lincoln should have done for advice on how to run the war.

- Lincoln's army was having a very difficult time at the beginning of the war. Ask students if they think this was due to poor leadership or a weak army. Have them support their answers.

- Ask students to meet in small groups and draft a letter of advice to Lincoln regarding what they think he should do about the slavery issue.

- Have students read the Emancipation Proclamation.

- Have students read the Gettysburg Address. Ask for volunteers to perform the speech in front of the class.

- Have students research the thirteenth amendment, which abolishes slavery. What does it say?

Amendment 13

[Slavery prohibited] Neither slavery nor involuntary servitude, except as a punishment for crime whereof the party shall have been duly convicted, shall exist within the United States or any place subject to their Jurisdiction.

- Lincoln took his young son Tad with him to examine a war torn area. Ask students if they think this was a good idea. Have them give their reasons.

- Lincoln's bodyguard left to watch the play while he was supposed to be watching Lincoln. As a result, Lincoln was shot and killed. Have students hold a mock trial for both the bodyguard and Lincoln's assassin, John Wilkes Booth.

- Have students write a eulogy for Lincoln. Ask some students to perform their eulogy for the class.

- When Lincoln died all the personal belongings that were on him at the time were placed in a box and sealed. The box was marked "Do not open." Ask students why they think this box may have been marked in such a way.

- On pages 133-137 of *Lincoln: A Photobiography* are selected quotes from Lincoln. Have students select a quote and respond to it in writing.

Situation Wanted!

Lincoln needed to find a job after losing his bid for a seat in the State Legislature. He had some skills that certainly someone could benefit from. When people seek a certain situation, they can place an ad in the "situation wanted" section of the classifieds. Write a "situation wanted" ad for Lincoln to place in his local newspaper.

CLASSIFIED
SITUATION WANTED

_____

_____

_____

_____

_____

_____

_____

_____

_____

_____

_____

_____

_____

_____

_____

_____

_____

_____

_____

North vs. South

The North and South were violently opposed to each other over the issue of slavery. The South had specific reasons for which they felt slavery was necessary. The North had their own reasons for opposing it. Using the information from Lincoln's story, note the arguments for each side of the slavery issue.

Contrast Chart

Arguments against slavery by the North	Arguments for slavery by the South

Civil War Bibliography

Alcott, Louisa May. *Little Women*. (Little, Brown, 1968)

Angle, Paul. *A Pictorial History of the Civil War*. (Doubleday, 1980)

Beatty, Patricia. *Be Ever Hopeful, Hannalee*. (Morrow, 1988)

Beatty, Patricia. *Charley Skedaddle*. (Morrow, 1987)

Beatty, Patricia. *Jayhawker*. (Morrow, 1991)

Carter, Alden. *Civil War: American Tragedy*. (Watts, 1992)

Clapp, Patricia. *The Tamarack Tree*. (Lothrop, 1986)

Climo, Shirley. *Month of Seven Days*. (HarperCollins, 1987)

Coffey, Vincent. *The Battle of Gettysburg*. (Burdett, 1985)

Coit, Margaret. *The Fight for Union*. (Houghton Mifflin, 1961)

Cosner, S. *War Nurses*. (Walker, 1988)

Erdman, L. G. *Save Weeping for the Night*. (Dodd, Mead, 1975)

Garrison, Webb. *Civil War Trivia and Fact Book*. (Rutledge Hill Press, 1992)

Hansen, Joyce. *Out from this Place*. (Walker, 1988)

Hoobler, D., and T. Hoobler. *Photographing History: The Career of Mathew Brady*. (Putnam, 1977)

Hunt, Irene. *Across Five Aprils*. (Follett, 1964)

Hurmence, Belinda. *Tancy*. (Clarion, 1984)

Kantor, MacKinlay. *Gettysburg*. (Random, 1963)

Kassem, Lou. *Listen for Rachel*. (Macmillan, 1986)

Keith, Harold. *Rifles for Watie*. (Harper, 1987)

Kent, Zachary. *Story of the Battle of Bull Run*. (Childrens Press, 1986)

Kent, Zachary. *Story of Sherman's March to the Sea*. (Childrens Press, 1987)

Kent, Zachary. *Story of the Surrender at Appomattox Court House*. (Childrens Press, 1988)

Kent, Zachary. *Ulysses S. Grant*. (Childrens Press, 1989)

Melzter, M. (Ed). *Voices from the Civil War: A Documentary History of the Great American Conflict*. (Crowell, 1989)

O'Dell, Scott. *Sing Down the Moon*. (Houghton Mifflin, 1970)

Perez, N. A. *The Slopes of War*. (Houghton Mifflin, 1984)

Ray, D. *The Story of How the Civil War Began*. (Dutton, 1990)

Reeder, C. *Shades of Gray*. (Macmillan, 1989)

Reit, Seymour. *Behind Rebel Lines*. (Harcourt, 1988)

Rickerby, Laura. *Ulysses S. Grant & the Strategy of Victory*. (Silver Burdett, 1990)

Robertson, James Jr. *Civil War: America Becomes One Nation*. (Knopf, 1992)

Stone, Melissa. *Clouds of War*. (Steck-Vaughn, 1989)

Weidhorn, M. *Robert E. Lee*. (Atheneum, 1988)

Winter, Jeanette. *Follow the Drinking Gourd*. (Knopf, 1988)

Wisler, Clifton. *Thunder on the Tennessee*. (Lodestar, 1983)

Hero Over Here: A Story of World War I

Author: Kathleen V. Kudinski

Illustrator: Bert Dodson

Publisher: Penguin, New York, 1990. 54 pages

Summary: This book tells a story about a young boy who learns that war heroes are not just those who fight, but also those who must stay home and take care of the family.

Learning Activities:

(Chapters 1-3)

- Theo thought that in order to be a hero you must fight in a war and come home with many medals. Have students brainstorm their ideas of what a hero is. Then have them write an essay about what being a hero means to them.

- Allow students to sing "Over There."

- Theo is pleased with his gift from Miss O'Reiley. She gave him a travel poster advertising travel by train to the West. Have students develop a travel brochure to go along with the poster from Miss O'Reiley.

- When Theo's older brother goes off to war there is some question as to who will be in charge at the house. Have students debate whether Theo should be in charge because he is now the only "man of the house" or if Irene should be in charge because she is now the oldest child in the house.

- Theo tries to imagine the battles in France that he reads about in the newspapers. Have students research some of the World War I battles in France. Then have them write a newspaper story about one of the battles.

- When George's mother dies, Theo feels very bad. However, it is hard for him to talk about how he feels. Have students write a letter of condolence to George from Theo expressing the feelings he is unable to talk about.

Hero Over Here: A Story of World War I *(cont.)*

- Have students predict Theo's family's fate.
- The flu epidemic of 1918 was very serious. Have students research this epidemic. Then have them write a brief report of their findings. For extra credit, have them research other epidemics.

(Chapters 4-6)

- As more and more people die from the flu epidemic, old family health secrets are used to fight the disease. Some involved hanging sheets soaked in vinegar; others, putting hot fried onions on the sick person's back. Some people even ate hot pepper sandwiches. As a class, discuss any old family health secrets that students may know about. See if there are any scientific connections in the remedies that students suggest.
- Now that both Irene and his mother are very sick, Theo is in charge of the house. Have students discuss how they think Theo feels about being in charge under these circumstances. Does he appreciate the challenge and responsibility, or does he wish someone else were in charge?
- Theo went out of his way to help a sick, homeless man even though his own family was badly in need of help. Ask students why they think Theo cared so much for this sick man.

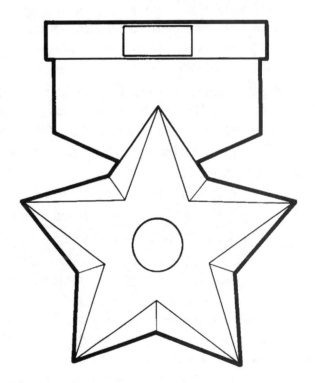

- The policeman who found Theo taking the sick man to the hospital was impressed with his fortitude. Have students create a special award for Theo from the police department honoring his citizenship.
- Have students predict what the fate of the sick man will be.
- The story ends without us knowing the fate of Theo's older brother, Everett. Have students predict what will happen to Everett.
- Have students write an essay responding to whether or not they think Theo is a hero.

Sadako and the Thousand Paper Cranes

Author: Eleanor Coerr

Paintings By: Ronald Himler

Publisher: Putnam, New York, 1977. 64 pages

Summary: Sadako was only two years old when the atom bomb was dropped on Hiroshima where she lived with her family. Ten years later Sadako has leukemia as a result of the radiation from the bomb. Her only hope is to make 1,000 paper cranes which, according to a legend, will make her well again.

Learning Activities:

- In Sadako's culture, spiders and a cloudless day are signs of good luck. Challenge students to list what are considered good luck signs in their culture.

- Sadako was very excited to celebrate Peace Day on August 6th. Have students research this Japanese holiday and write a brief report.

- A cherished object in Sadako's house was the gold-framed picture of her grandmother in her kimono. Have students draw what they think Sadako's grandmother looked like and frame it with either gold construction paper or white construction paper sprinkled with gold glitter.

- Challenge students to find out more about leukemia. They can try to answer the following questions:

    What are the causes of leukemia?

    Can people in the United States get leukemia?

    Is there now a cure for leukemia?

- Sadako loved to run relays. Most children in the United States also love relay races. Have students organize relay races for their next physical education class period.

- Have students discuss whether or not they think it was appropriate to give Sadako false hope of survival if she made the thousand paper cranes.

- Sadako had made over 600 paper cranes before she died. Challenge students to make the additional cranes needed to reach 1000. Directions can be found on page 119. Before they begin, explain that origami is the ancient Asian art of paper folding. At one time it was believed that paper contained spirits and could not be cut. Before they fold the cranes they may wish to practice with the simpler design on page 120.

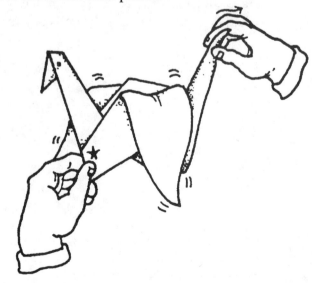

One Thousand Cranes

Sadako made over 600 paper cranes before she died. You and your classmates are challenged to make the other 400 cranes for a total of 1000. Directions to make the origami crane are detailed below.

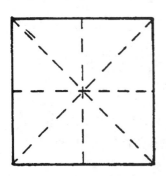

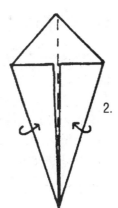

1. Fold your square four times as shown below.

2. Using a diagonal fold as the center, fold the left and right edges into the center line to make a kite shape.

3. Repeat kite fold on each corner. Your opened paper should be creased as shown.

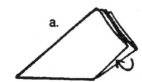

4. Fold the paper in half to make a triangle. Hold it at the star and fold the right side up to meet the top of the triangle.

5. Release the fold and make the same fold inside out, with the fold coming between the front and back of the large triangle. Repeat on left side. Sharpen the crease.

  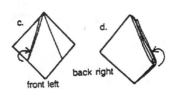 

front right   front left   back right   back left

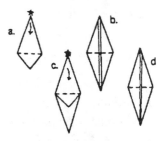

6. Hold the point with the star and fold down the top flap at the broken line. Turn the shape over and repeat the fold on the other side.

7. Fold down the right flap at the broken line. Release and make the same fold inside out. Repeat on the left side.

 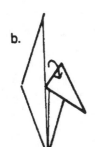 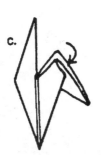

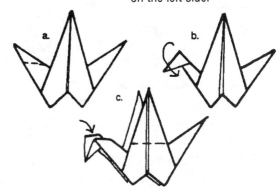

8. Turn the shape as shown and fold the end of the point at the broken line to form the crane's head. Release and make the same fold inside out. Fold down the top flap at the broken line to make a wing. Turn over and fold the other wing.

9. Roll the wings around a pencil to give a curved shape.

Other Origami Fun

Origami is the ancient Asian art of paper folding. At one time it was believed that paper contained spirits and could not be cut. Follow these directions to make an origami boat. Enjoy!

How to Make a Floating Boat

This paper boat will not last long. You can float this boat in the sink, in the bath, or even in a bucket of water.

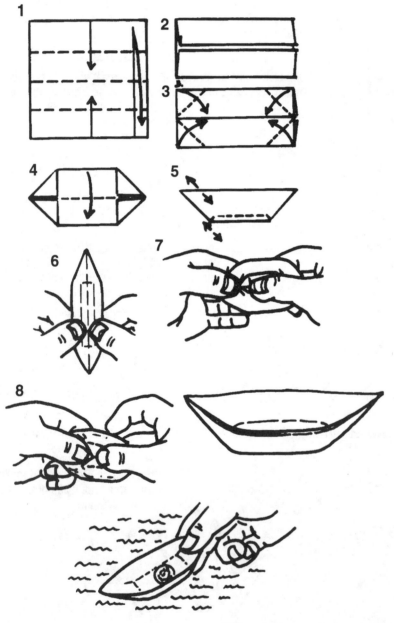

1. Hold the paper vertically. Fold the paper in half.

2. Open the paper and fold both ends of the paper inward to the middle fold. Make sure the ends touch, but do not overlap.

3. Turn the paper over and fold the four corners.

4. Fold in half.

5. Pull the layers apart at the top, by opening two layers to one side and one layer to the other.

6. Press on the bottom to form the shape of the boat.

7. Turn over and make a crease across the seam at one end with one thumb and flatten the point with the other thumb. Do the same thing at the other end.

8. Round out the boat and raise the sides to complete.

Floating Your Boat

One side of the boat will be heavier than the other and the boat will tip to the heavier side. To steady your boat, place a coin or two on the lighter side of the boat. You may or may not need to tape the pennies onto the boat.

The Bracelet

Author: Yoshiko Uchida

Illustrator: Joanna Yardley

Publisher: Philomel, New York, 1993.
28 pages

Summary: Emi and her sister have lived alone with their mother ever since their father was taken away by the FBI because he worked for a Japanese company. Now the family is forced to live in a Japanese internment camp until the war ends. Emi, however, is able to gain strength and hope from the special bracelet her best friend Laurie gave her before she left for the camp.

Learning Activities:

- Have students in small groups discuss whether or not they think the United States was justified in placing the Japanese-Americans in internment camps because of the war.

- Have students write a thank-you note to Laurie from Emi for the special bracelet.

- Use the following question as a writing prompt for students. "Do you need something tangible in order to remember someone special?" Encourage students to predict what happened to Emi and her family when the war ended. Then ask students to write a new book about Emi and her family based on their predictions for the future.

- Emi's family was forced to make an old horse stall their home during their imprisonment. Have students brainstorm alternative types of houses (e.g. an igloo or a teepee). You may want to read *A House Is a House for Me* by Mary Ann Hoberman (Viking, 1978) to help spark students thinking.

- Have students make a list of tangible things that remind them of a certain person. Use the activity sheet on page 122.

- Allow students to make special friendship bracelets using colorful string and square knots as pictured below.

Special Memories

The bracelet reminds Emi of her best friend Laurie. On the activity sheet below, list objects that remind you of a certain person and why they remind you of that person.

Object	Person of who I am reminded	Special Memory

My Daddy Was a Soldier

Author and Illustrator: Deborah Kogan Ray

Publisher: Holiday House, New York, 1990. 40 pages

Summary: Jeanne and her mother learn to survive on their own after her father is sent to be in the war. Their only joy is derived from the letters they receive from father while he is away.

Learning Activities:

- Have students give a radio report of the bombings and battles as described in the story.

- The reader is not privy to the conversation between the mother and father before he leaves for war. Have students write this conversation as they think it may have gone. Then, students may dramatize the conversation if they wish.

- Have students write the letter Jeanne received from her father.

- Have students make a special card from Jeanne to send to her father.

- Food was rationed during the war. Explain to students that this was because the needs of the soldiers came before the needs of the consumer on the home front. Have students discuss in small groups what they think the rations of milk, meat, cheese, canned goods, and vegetables should be for a family of four for a period of one month. (The book *V is for Victory* by Sylvia Whitman, Lerner, 1992 has some excellent information to share about rationing.)

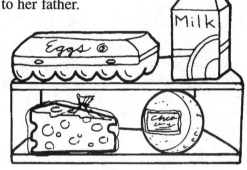

- When sugar was no longer available, Jeanne put corn syrup on her cornflakes. Allow students to try what this tastes like.

- Either at school or at home, have students plant a small victory garden of peas, beans, tomatoes, or other vegetables.

- Have students create a pencil drawing of Jeanne's dad in his uniform.

- Using the special design on page 124, have students design the special award Jeanne and Carol won for their efforts in the scrap drive.

- Have students design the medals of bravery Jeanne's father won.

Super "Scrap Drive" Winners

Design the special award that Jeanne and Carol received for winning the "scrap drive."

124

Number the Stars

Author: Lois Lowry

Publisher: Houghton Mifflin, Boston, 1989. 132 pages

Summary: In this Newbery Award-winning classic, Annemarie and her family must protect their Jewish friends as the German soldiers take over Copenhagen, Denmark. Annemarie, while quite young, turns out to be a real hero in the story by saving her best friend and her family.

Learning Activities:

(Chapters 1-4)

- Annemarie and Ellen practiced running for the races they planned to participate in at school. Students can have races either at recess or during physical education period.

- Have students locate Copenhagen, Denmark on a world map. You can use a map in your classroom or the map located in page 144. Ask questions such as where Denmark is in relationship to the United States and Germany. What oceans would you have to cross to get to Copenhagen from the United States?

- Throughout the story, have students keep a dialectical journal of their responses. In a dialectical journal, students choose a quote from the story that is particularly meaningful or powerful to them. They write this quote on one side of the page. On the other half of the page, they write their response to the quote. It would be set up something like this:

Book Quote	Your Response
Annemarie knew instantly which photographs he had chosen.	I was curious to find out which pictures were chosen.

- The children in Denmark are all familiar with the fairy tales of Hans Christian Anderson because he is from Denmark. Have students choose their favorite Anderson fairy tale to read to a child in another grade level. Perhaps this can be arranged with a first or second grade teacher at your school.

- Using the world map located in the appendix of this book, have students locate all the countries that were occupied by German soldiers.

Number the Stars *(cont.)*

- Once the Germans took over, there was an 8:00 p.m. curfew. Ask students why they think there was such a curfew. Then ask them what their own curfew is and whether or not they think it is a fair time.

- Have students do a personality profile of Annemarie and Ellen. What do they know about them from the book? What can they infer about their personalities? Are either of them brave?

- Have students do research on Hitler and why he wanted to "relocate" the Jews. Then, have them write a brief report of what they learned during the course of their research.

- Ellen really had a flair for the dramatic, as probably some of your own students do. Have students turn any scene from the book into a reader's theater script. In reader's theater, there are no props or scenery and no memorization of lines. Students simply read the lines directly from the script. You could divide the class so that half of the students write the script and the other half are the performers.

- Since the German occupation, the people in Denmark have been running out of food and supplies. For example; sugar, butter, and leather are nonexistent. Ask students if they were placed in a similar situation what items they would miss most from their lives.

- Kirsti remembers seeing fireworks on one of her birthdays. Although it was really a battle, her parents prefer that she believe it was fireworks. Have students do a crayon resist of a fireworks scene by following the directions below.

  Materials: fluorescent crayons, construction paper, dark blue watercolor paints

  1. Using fluorescent crayons, have students draw explosive fireworks on a piece of construction paper.
  2. Using dark blue watercolors, paint over the entire piece of construction paper.
  3. The crayons will resist the paint when it dries, making the fireworks scene stand out.

- Kirsti loves stories about kings and queens. Have students write a story involving a king or queen that would be appropriate for Annemarie to tell Kirsti.

Number the Stars *(cont.)*

(Chapters 5-9)

- Ellen wants to be an actress when she grows up but her father wants her to be a teacher like himself. Ask students what they want to be as adults. Then ask them if their parents have put any pressure on their decision.

- Annemarie's father proved to the soldiers that Ellen was their daughter by showing them a picture. After seeing the picture, the soldier tore it up. Ask students why they think the soldier would have done such a thing.

- Have students predict what would have happened if the German soldiers had figured out that Ellen was not Annemarie's sister.

- Annemarie's mother enjoyed hearing ghost stories when she was a little girl. Allow students to tell their favorite ghost stories to the class. If you wish to share some stories, a good resource is *Short and Shivery* by Robert D. San Souci (Doubleday, 1987).

- Have students draw a picture of Henrik's house using the descriptions provided in the novel. They may also wish to use their imagination to fill in some details.

- It was a real treat to have applesauce at a time when food was so scarce. Have students make applesauce using the recipe below.

Applesauce

Ingredients: 2 ½ pounds (114 kg) apples cut into quarters, sugar to taste, cinnamon

Directions: Place quartered apples in saucepan and cover partly with water. Simmer apples until tender. Blend apples together and put through a strainer. Return applesauce to saucepan and add sugar to taste. Sprinkle with cinnamon when ready to serve. Makes about 1 quart (960mL).

- Have students discuss in small groups what bravery means to them. Then have them write a personal story in which they think they displayed bravery.

- As a class, discuss if it is easier to be brave when you do not know everything.

Number the Stars *(cont.)*

- Annemarie and Ellen collected dried flowers to decorate Uncle Henrik's house. Students can make dried flowers using these directions.

   Materials: fresh cut flowers, nails, string, scissors, a warm, dry, dark place to hang flowers

   1. Cut the flowers before they are in full bloom and remove leaves.
   2. Group flowers together using string to tie stems together. Do not bunch too tightly because the air needs to circulate in order to dry the blossoms.
   3. Hang flowers upside down suspended from a nail in a warm, dry, dark place for three to five weeks.

(Chapters 10-17)

- Have students discuss why Annemarie's family did not try to go to Sweden considering the circumstances.
- Have students write a good-bye letter to Annemarie from Ellen.
- Let your students imagine that the Germans found out Peter was with the resistance movement. Working together in small groups, have them create a wanted poster for Peter.
- Have students make predictions on the following questions:

   What would have happened to Annemarie if the soldiers figured out the plan regarding the handkerchief?

   What is the Rosen's life like in Sweden?

   Will the Rosens ever come back to live in Copenhagen?

- Have students research and draw the Danish flag.

- Peter wrote the Johansen family a final letter before he died. What did this letter say? Have students draft what they think this letter may have said.
- Annemarie never considered herself to be a brave person. Have students detail her heroic actions using the activity sheet on page 129.

Annemarie: Our Heroine

In spite of everything Annemarie did to help her friends, the Rosens, she still did not feel as though she was brave. Using the chart below, chronicle all the brave, heroic actions Annemarie performed during the course of the story. Then answer the question that follows on a separate piece of paper.

Annemarie's Bravery Chart

Chapters	Brave Actions
1-3	
4-6	
7-9	
10-12	
13-16	

Do you think Annemarie is brave? _____

_____

World Wars Bibliography

Bauer, M. D. *Rain of Fire.* (Clarion, 1983)

Bernbaum, I. *My Brother's Keeper: The Holocaust Through the Eyes of an Artist.* (Putnam, 1985)

Chaikin, M. *A Nightmare in History: The Holocaust.* (Clarion, 1987)

Davis, D. S. *Behind Barbed Wire: The Imprisonment of Japanese Americans During World War II.* (Dutton, 1982)

Devaney, J. *America Goes to War.* (Walker, 1991)

Frank, Anne. *Anne Frank: The Diary of a Young Girl.* (Pocket Books, 1952)

Hahn, M. D. *Stepping on the Cracks.* (Clarion, 1991)

Innocenti, R., and C. Gallaz. *Rose Blanche.* (Creative Education, 1985)

Kerr, Judith. *When Hitler Stole Pink Rabbit.* (Coward, 1972)

Landau, E. *We Survived the Holocaust.* (Watts, 1991)

Marrin, A. *The Airman's War: World War II.* (Atheneum, 1982)

Maruki, T. *Hiroshima No Pika.* (Lothrop, 1980)

McSwigan, Marie. *Snow Treasure.* (Dutton, 1942)

Orlev, Uri. *The Island on Bird Street.* (Houghton Mifflin, 1984)

Reiss, Johanna. *The Upstairs Room.* (Harper, 1972)

Rogasky, B. *Smoke and Ashes: The Story of the Holocaust.* (Holiday House, 1988)

Rostkowski, M. L. *After the Dancing Days.* (Harper, 1986)

Sachs, Marilyn. *A Pocket Full of Seeds.* (Doubleday, 1973)

Schellie, D. *Shadow and the Gunner.* (Four Winds, 1982)

Sender, R. M. *To Life.* (Macmillan, 1988)

Uchida, Yoshiko. *Journey to Topaz.* (Creative Arts, 1971)

Yolen, Jane. *All Those Secrets of the World.* (Little, Brown, 1991)

Yolen, Jane. *The Devil's Arithmetic.* (Viking, 1988)

Park's Quest

Author: Katherine Paterson

Publisher: Dutton, New York, 1988.
148 pages

Summary: There has always been a great deal of secrecy surrounding Park's father's life. His mother never wants to discuss his father, who was killed in the Vietnam War. Frustrated, Park is determined to find out about his father. Unfortunately, he doesn't quite find out what he wants to hear.

Learning Activities:

(Chapters 1-4)

- Park was very concerned about the time zone difference between the United States and Vietnam. Have students find out the difference and then practice math skills by calculating what time it would be in Vietnam if it were a certain time in the United States.

- Have students imagine that they are a part of a child rights' advocacy group. Then, ask them to write a speech on Park's behalf regarding his rights to find out about his father.

- Park is very interested in poetry. He is particularly intrigued by a selection his mother noted about a very happy time and a very sad time. Have students find two poems, one that describes a sad time for them and one that describes a happy time. You may even wish to have students write these poems themselves.

- Park thinks you can learn a lot about people by knowing what types of books they read. Make a class graph or chart listing favorite books. Then, challenge students to decide what types of people read certain types of books for example, science fiction, mystery, or romance novels.

- Park's mother writes a letter to his father's family requesting permission for Park to visit. Have students write the letter from Park's mother.

- Have students find out more about the Vietnam Memorial in Washington D.C.. Let them research and find some pictures of it and then paint a mural of the Vietnam Memorial Wall that Park had the opportunity to visit.

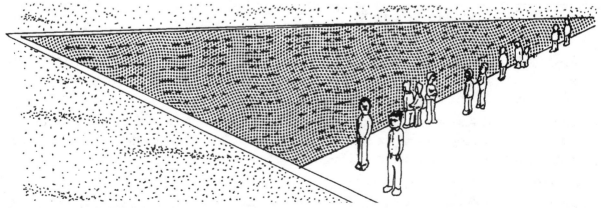

Park's Quest *(cont.)*

(Chapters 5-9)

- Have students draw a picture of the Broughton family mansion and the bedroom Park will be staying in. The book provides rich descriptions of both.

- In chapter six Park meets Thanh for the first time. Their relationship is stormy throughout the novel, but it does go through some basic changes. Have students keep a journal of the changes in the relationship between Thanh and Park as the story progresses.

- Mrs. Davenport is a tough one to figure out. Have students make a list of the characters Mrs. Davenport is in contact with and then a brief description of what she really thinks of each character.

- Park had a difficult time learning how to milk a cow. In small groups have students discuss something that was difficult for them to learn the very first time they tried it. Ask them to discuss how their own experience was similar to Park's experience with the cows.

- In small groups have students discuss the following questions:

    Why was the grandfather crying all the time?

    Should Park have asked to learn to shoot when he knows his mother would disapprove?

    Why is Thanh so mean to Park?

    Why is Frank hesitant to let Park meet the Colonel?

- Biscuits are about the only thing Park enjoys eating when Mrs. Davenport is doing the cooking. Allow students to make biscuits and serve them to the class. Several recipes can be found in *The Little House Cookbook* by Barbara M. Walker (HarperCollins, 1979).

- The reader only knows what the grandfather is like after having suffered from two strokes. Have students write a biography of the grandfather's life prior to having his first stroke. They can use details from the story and their own imagination.

- Have students discuss what Thanh's life may have been like when she was living in Vietnam.

Park's Quest (cont.)

(Chapters 10-14)

- Have students imagine that the grandfather can talk. What would he say to Thanh and Park after his wild ride? Have students write and perform this conversation.

- Park was smart enough to figure out that he and Thanh were brother and sister. This is where the story and the character relationships get a little confusing. To help sort things out, have students draw a Broughton family tree using the information found throughout the story.

- The reader is left wondering what happens between Park and his mom when he finally returns home. Have students write a final chapter to this story in which Park has returned home to his mother.

- Thanh and Park are different, yet similar. Have students complete the interest inventory for each character on page 134 and 135. Then, have students draw portraits of each character using page 136. This will help them discover with greater depth each of these complex characters.

- Have students discuss the following questions in small groups:

  Why did Frank marry Thanh's mom?

  Why was Park blaming himself for the bad situation at the Broughton house?

  Was Park's mother right in trying to protect him from the truth?

  Do you think Park will ever visit the Memorial again?

- Have students imagine that Park is able to somehow contact his father. Then have students make a list of the questions they think Park would ask his father.

- Have students predict what Thanh and Park's relationship will be like in ten years.

- Have students write the grandfather's will. To whom will he leave each of his possessions?

Park and Thanh: Alike or Different?

Fill out the interest inventory below as you think Park Broughton would. Then fill out the interest inventory on the following page as you think Thanh would.

Interest Inventory for Park

1. Three things I like are: _____

    _____

    _____

2. Three things I dislike are: _____

    _____

    _____

    _____

3. The best thing about me is: _____

    _____

4. When I grow up I want to be: _____

5. My favorites are:

    animal_____

    type of book _____

    color _____

    food_____

    hobby _____

    toy_____

    sport _____

6. Draw a self-portrait of Park using page 136.

Park and Thanh, Alike or Different *(cont.)*

Now fill out the interest inventory below as you think Thanh would.

Interest inventory for Thanh:

1. Three things I like are: _____

   _____

   _____

2. Three things I dislike are: _____

   _____

   _____

3. The best thing about me is: _____

   _____

4. When I grow up I want to be: _____

5. My favorites are:

   animal _____

   type of book _____

   color _____

   food _____

   hobby _____

   toy _____

   sport _____

6. Draw a self-portrait of Thanh using page 136.

Park and Thanh, Alike or Different *(cont.)*

Use this page to draw individual portraits of Park and Thanh.

A Wall of Names

Author: Judy Donnelly

Publisher: Random House, New York, 1991. 48 pages

Summary: This book is an easy-to-read story of the funding and building of the Vietnam Veteran's Memorial.

Learning Activities:

- As students read about the Memorial, have them make a memorial bulletin board.
- Locate Vietnam on a map for students. You can use the world map on page 144.
- The idea of the Vietnam Memorial did not win the support of everyone. Some felt we should just try to forget about that war. Hold a debate in class with students representing both sides of the argument.

- Invite a Vietnam veteran to the class to speak and answer questions. Prepare students for this visit by having them prepare questions in advance.
- The television brought reports of the war into the households of Americans. Have students write a brief news report based on the information from the book or independent research. It should be a brief report, no more than three to five minutes long, and it should be delivered like a real news cast.
- At one large protest, each person carried a candle for a soldier that had died in the war. Have students make candles as memorials by following the directions for candle making on page 57 of this book.
- Have students write a newspaper article describing the protest of the war in which two students were killed. They should be encouraged to do independent research to obtain more facts about the protest.
- Have students write an impassioned speech for Jan Scruggs to give to people he is trying to solicit donations from for the Memorial.

A Wall of Names *(cont.)*

- Have students create a poster announcing the opening of the Vietnam Veteran Memorial.

- Jan Scruggs worked very hard to make the Memorial a reality. Have students write Jan a thank-you letter for his efforts.

- Another way to honor Jan Scruggs would be to create a special award for him. Have students design and create this special award.

- Some people felt that the Memorial Wall was not enough. They wanted a statue. So, there was a compromise and a statue was built along with the Memorial Wall. A picture of the statue is located on page 5 of *A Wall of Names.* Have students make a clay statue similar to the one pictured in the book.

- Have students discuss what they think of the way the soldiers were treated when they returned from Vietnam.

- Many people leave flowers in front of the Memorial as a tribute. Have students make tissue paper flowers by following the directions below. These flowers can be placed on the Vietnam Memorial bulletin board.

  Materials: one 9" x 12" (23 cm x 30 cm) sheet of white construction paper for each student, green watercolors or markers, glue, scissors, pencil, colored tissue paper

  1. On the construction paper, draw an outline of a few flowers complete with stems and leaves. Leave a 1" (2.54 cm) border around the paper.

  2. Color stems and leaves with green markers or watercolors.

  3. Cut colored paper into circles about the size of a half dollar. The circles will serve as petals for each flower. Make five or six circles for each flower.

  4. To form a petal, evenly cover the end of a pencil with a tissue paper circle and pull up around the pencil. Dip the tissue circle lightly in glue and place the petal on the flower drawing. Continue gluing petals to flowers.

  5. Make a 3-D frame by folding in the construction paper about 1" (2.54 cm) along the edges. Tape, staple, or glue the corners together.

Always to Remember

Author: Brent Ashabranner

Photographs: Jennifer Ashabranner

Publisher: Putnam, New York, 1988.
92 pages

Summary: This book tells the story of Jan Scruggs, the Vietnam Veteran determined to have a national memorial for those who fought in the Vietnam War. Photographs of the memorial at every stage during its building accompany the story.

Learning Activities:

(Chapters 1-3)

- Encourage students to find out more about the origin of Memorial Day. A good resource book is *Celebration: The Story of American Holidays* by Lucille Recht Penner (Macmillan, 1993).

- Have students respond in writing to the tribute inscribed on one of the center panels of the Vietnam Memorial Wall, "Our nation honors the courage, sacrifice, and devotion to duty and country of its Vietnam veterans."

- People often leave floral wreaths at the Memorial Wall. Have students make Memorial wreaths that could be used to decorate a bulletin board tribute to Vietnam veterans. Directions are listed below for making inexpensive wreaths.

    Materials: elbow or shell macaroni, glue, paper plates, spray paint
    1. Cut out center of paper plate.
    2. Glue macaroni to paper plate. Let dry overnight.
    3. Spray paint desired color.

Always to Remember (cont.)

- Locate Vietnam on a map for students. You can use the world map on page 144.

- At the time of the beginning of the Vietnam War many recent high school graduates were joining the army rather than going to college. Have students meet in small groups to talk about their future career plans.

- Jan Scruggs became obsessed with the idea of a Vietnam Memorial because it was so important to him. Have students write about something that was so important to them that they became obsessed with the idea.

- Have students write the speech they think Jan Scruggs gave at his press conference introducing his idea of a Vietnam Memorial.

- Have students discuss the following questions in small groups:

  Why did the young boy leave a marble at the Vietnam Memorial?

  Is it appropriate to read the messages others have left at the Memorial?

  Why were the Vietnam soldiers treated so poorly upon their return?

  Is it possible to distinguish between the war and those who fought it?

(Chapters 4-9)

- Have students create their own design for the Vietnam Memorial that they would have entered in the contest.

- Maya was very excited to receive the phone call from Washington telling her that she had won the contest. Have students write this phone conversation as they think it may have gone. Others can perform the conversation if they wish.

- Have students design an announcement for the dedication ceremony of the Memorial.

- The five-day Memorial ceremony for the dedication of the Wall included a candlelight vigil. Students can make candles by following the directions on page 57 of this book. Then they can hold a mock vigil to pay respect to the Vietnam veterans.

Always to Remember (cont.)

- Victoria Richards made an enormous flag out of red, white, and blue flowers. Have students make flags out of tissue paper following the directions below.

    Materials: red, white, and blue tissue paper; glue; a pencil; rectangular piece of construction paper.

    1. Draw an outline of the flag on the piece of construction paper.

    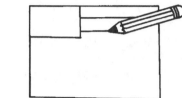

    2. Fill in the flag using the appropriate colors of tissue paper. This is done by wrapping the tissue paper around the eraser tip of the pencil, then dipping the tip in glue. The tissue is then placed on the construction paper.

    3. When they finish, have students write a brief statement of respect to accompany the flag. Flags can then be placed on a bulletin board display.

- Have students draft a thank-you letter to Victoria Richards from a Vietnam veteran who was at the dedication ceremony and appreciated the special floral flag.

- Have students design a special award or certificate for Jan Scruggs for his determination in getting the Memorial Wall built.

- After doing some research about the life of Jan Scruggs, have students write a complete biography. Details about the struggle to have the Vietnam Wall built should be emphasized.

- Have students make a diorama of the Constitution Gardens and the Vietnam Wall.

- As a tribute to Vietnam veterans let students write poems for them. Before beginning make sure students understand that there are many different types of poems to write. Some appropriate types of poems to use would include acrostic verse, cinquain, and diamante.

Vietnam War Bibliography

Barr, Roger. *Vietnam War.* (Lucent, 1991)

Black, Wallace & Jean F Blashfield. *War Behind the Lines.* (Macmillan, 1992)

Boyd, Candy D. *Charlie Pippin.* (Macmillan, 1987)

Carn, John B. *Vietnam Blues.* (Holloway, 1988)

Fincher, E. B. *The Vietnam War.* (Watts, 1980)

Hahn, Mary, D. *December Stillness.* (Clarion, 1988)

Hauptly, D. J. *In Vietnam.* (Atheneum, 1985)

Hoobler, D., and T. Hoobler. *Vietnam: An Illustrated History.* (Knopf, 1990)

Hoobler, D., and T. Hoobler. *Vietnam: Why We Fought.* (Knopf, 1990)

Jacobson, Karen. *Vietnam.* (Childrens, 1992)

Lawson, D. *An Album of the Vietnam War.* (Watts, 1986)

Maynard Christopher. *War Vehicles.* (Lerner, 1980)

Myers, Walter Dean. *Fallen Angels.* (Scholastic, 1988)

Nelson, Theresa. *And One for All.* (Orchard, 1989)

Nhong, Huynh Quang. *The Land I Lost.* (HarperCollins, 1986)

Nhong, Huynh Quang. *The Land I Lost: Adventures of a Boy in Vietnam.* (Lippincott, 1982)

Warren, J. *Portrait of a Tragedy: America and the Vietnam War.* (Lothrop, 1990)

Williams, Brian. *War and Weapons.* (Random, 1987)

Wolitzer, M. *Caribou.* (Greenwillow, 1984)

Wright, David K. *War in Vietnam Bks I-IV.* (Childrens Press, 1989)

United States Map

World Map

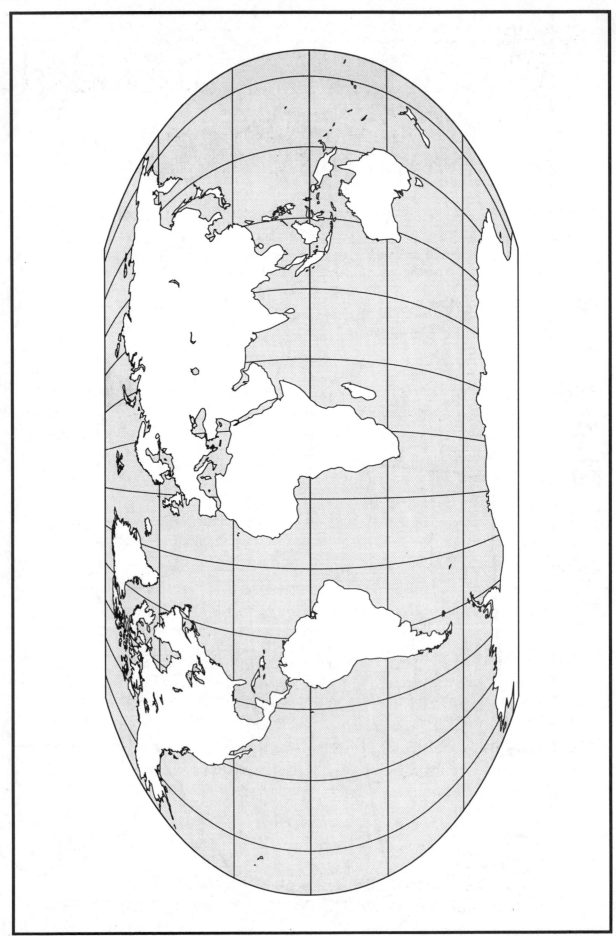